A PILGRIMAGE IN PRAYER

FORTY DAYS WITH THE VIRGIN MARY

William Gomes

Copyright © 2024 William Gomes

All rights reserved. No part of this publication may be reproduced or transmitted in any form or by any means, electronic or mechanical, including photocopying, recording, or any information storage or retrieval system, without prior permission in writing from the publishers.

Dedication

This book is lovingly dedicated to all who have been touched by the gentle and transformative Gaze of Mary. May the words within these pages serve as a reminder of her enduring presence and guiding light, leading you closer to the embrace of divine love.

Table of Contents

Introduction: 1

Day 1: Embracing Humility with Mary 5

Day 2: Finding Strength in Faith 7

Day 3: The Joy of God's Promise 9

Day 4: Walking in Faith with Mary 11

Day 5: The Light of God's Grace 14

Day 6: Trusting in God's Timing 16

Day 7: The Compassion of Mary 19

Day 8: Mary's Role as Intercessor 21

Day 9: Embracing God's Peace Through Mary 24

Day 10: Mary's Faithfulness Through Trials 26

Day 11: Mary's Quiet Contemplation 29

Day 12: Mary as the First Disciple 31

Day 13: Mary's Journey of Faith..33

Day 14: Mary's Heart of Service..36

Day 15: Finding Strength in Mary's Faith 39

Day 16: Mary's Example of Listening 41

Day 17: Mary's Witness to Joy 44

Day 18: Emulating Mary's Patience 47

Day 19: Mary's Role as a Mother to All 50

Day 20: Mary's Solace in Sorrow 52

Day 21: Mary as a Beacon of Hope 54
Day 22: Mary's Unwavering Faith 57
Day 23: Mary's Compassionate Heart 60
Day 24: Mary's Role in Divine Mercy 62
Day 25: Mary as the Model of Quiet Strength 64
Day 26: Mary, Model of Perseverance 66
Day 27: Mary, Our Guide in Prayer 69
Day 28: Mary's Intercession in Our Lives 72
Day 29: Embracing Mary's Humility 75
Day 30: Mary's Faithful Obedience 77
Day 31: Mary's Journey of Faith 79
Day 32: Mary's Loving Presence in Times of Need 81
Day 33: Mary as a Beacon of Hope 83
Day 34: Mary's Compassionate Heart 86
Day 35: Mary's Role as a Disciple 88
Day 36: Mary's Gaze of Love and Sorrow 90
Day 37: At the Foot of the Cross 93
Day 38: Mary's Faith Beyond the Cross 95
Day 39: Mary as the New Eve 97
Day 40: The Culmination of the Journey 99

Introduction

In the pages that follow, you are invited on a profound spiritual odyssey, one that I, William Gomes, have embarked upon, guided by the transformative Gaze of Mary. This journey, encapsulated within "A Pilgrimage in Prayer: Forty Days with the Virgin Mary," extends beyond the boundaries of a traditional devotional. It is a narrative of encounter, a testimony of transformation, and a bridge to a deeper communion with Jesus through the maternal affection and guidance of the Virgin Mary.

The essence of this pilgrimage is deeply rooted in my own life's narrative, where Mary's Gaze has shone as a beacon of divine grace amidst the tumultuous seas of marginalization, disability, forced migration, and persecution. It is a challenge to encapsulate the depth and breadth of Mary's Gaze—it represents the juncture where the divine embraces the human, where salvation history intertwines with personal strife, and where the promise of God's love meets the stark reality of human suffering.

For me, Mary's Gaze has been a living, dynamic presence—a constant invitation to cultivate a deeper, more personal relationship with Jesus. It has served as a gateway to understanding the profound nature of God's love, a love that has permeated every facet of my existence, transforming my pain into a testament of hope and grace. This Gaze has not only uplifted me in moments of despair but has also empowered me to see my own sufferings as a path to closer union with God.

This book, therefore, serves as a reflection of that transformative journey—an invitation to you, dear reader, to explore the pivotal role of Mary in guiding us closer to her Son. Through forty days of prayer, reflection, and scripture, this pilgrimage aims to immerse you in the wonder of Mary's role in our salvation and her enduring presence in our lives.

As we traverse each day, I will share with you my personal story of how Mary's Gaze has anchored me. From the depths of hardship to the summits of spiritual insight, her Gaze has been a source of unshakeable trust in God's divine plan. It has taught me to embrace suffering not as a form of punishment, but as a sacred sacrament—a means of drawing closer to the compassionate heart of Jesus. Even in the darkest moments, when all seemed lost, it was Mary's Gaze that reminded me of the presence of grace, encouraging me to persevere in faith and love.

This devotional journey is more than a mere series of reflections; it is an opportunity to witness the transformative power of Mary's Gaze in one's life. It is my heartfelt prayer that as you journey through these forty days, you will encounter Mary's Gaze as I have: as a source of comfort, inspiration, and profound connection to Jesus. May this pilgrimage inspire you to open your heart to the wonders of God's love, to the strength found in surrender, and to the joy of living under the protective mantle of the Virgin Mary.

However, this story isn't mine alone; it is a story that we share. Through daily prayers, scripture readings, and reflections, you are invited to explore your own unique relationship with God, drawing inspiration from Mary's unwavering faith and trust.

Each day of this journey adheres to a consistent format:

Opening Prayer: To set our intentions and open our hearts to divine wisdom.

Scripture Reading: To connect with God's Word, in light of Mary's journey and our own.

Reflection: To contemplate the day's theme, drawing parallels between Mary's life and our personal experiences.

Prayer of the Day: To seek Mary's intercession and God's guidance in our lives.

Spiritual Exercise: Practical suggestions for bringing the day's lessons into our lives, encouraging active faith and deeper trust in God.

Closing Prayer: To conclude our daily pilgrimage, entrusting ourselves to Mary's care and God's love.

This journey is meticulously designed to deepen your faith, inspire a closer relationship with Jesus, and cultivate a reflective, prayerful stance towards life's challenges. Each day presents an opportunity to uncover the transformative power of faith, guided by Mary's exemplary life.

As we navigate these forty days together, let us open our hearts to the profound lessons that Mary's life offers us. It is my sincere hope that this pilgrimage enriches your spiritual life, offering you comfort, inspiration, and a profound sense of connection to the divine.

We embark on this journey not as solitary pilgrims but accompanied by the loving Gaze of Mary, which guides us, sustains us, and ultimately leads us closer to her Son, Jesus. May this pilgrimage serve as a wellspring of renewal, deepening your faith and drawing you into an intimate relationship with Jesus and the Catholic Church. Through the Gaze of Mary, may we all find the path to deeper love, enduring hope, and transformative grace.

Welcome to "A Pilgrimage in Prayer: Forty Days with the Virgin Mary." Let us commence this journey with open hearts, ready to be transformed by the loving Gaze of Mary, which eternally seeks to draw us closer to her Son, in a profound communion of love and faith.

Day 1

Embracing Humility with Mary

Opening Prayer:

O Holy Spirit, Divine Illuminator, and Blessed Virgin Mary, Mother of the Redeemer, illuminate our path as we commence this sacred journey. Guide our thoughts and open our hearts, that we might receive the fullness of God's wisdom and love on this pilgrimage in prayer.

Scripture Reading:

"Then Mary said, 'Here am I, the servant of the Lord; let it be with me according to your word.' Then the angel departed from her."

Luke 1:38

Reflection:

In this profound moment of surrender, Mary exemplifies ultimate humility and obedience to God's will. Her simple yet powerful affirmation, "Here am I, the servant of the Lord," reveals a heart fully open to God's plan, regardless of her own fears or uncertainties. This act of faith is not a passive submission but a courageous acceptance of her role in salvation history. As we reflect on Mary's response, we are invited to consider our own readiness to serve God with humility. Where in your life is God calling you to say, "Let it be with me according to your word"? How can Mary's example of trust and humility inspire you to embrace God's will with open-hearted bravery?

Prayer of the Day:

Holy Mary, Mother of God, your unwavering faith and humility set a precedent for all believers. As you accepted God's call without hesitation, pray for us, that we may also respond to God with a resolute "yes," trusting in His divine plan. Help us to embody the humility and obedience you showed, finding strength in submission and joy in God's service. May your example lead us closer to your Son, Jesus Christ. Amen.

Spiritual Exercise:

Reflect upon areas in your life where you struggle to surrender to God's will. Consider journaling about these instances and how Mary's example of humility and trust in God might guide you towards a more open and accepting stance. Alternatively, offer a prayer for someone in your life, asking for the grace to serve them with humility and love, echoing Mary's service to God.

Closing Prayer:

We are grateful, Lord, for the gift of Mary, our mother and guide on this journey of faith. Through her example of humility and obedience, may we grow closer to you, embracing your will with open hearts and minds. Blessed Virgin Mary, watch over us, your children, as we seek to live in the light of your Son, Jesus, our Lord and saviour. Amen.

Day 2

Finding Strength in Faith

Opening Prayer:

O Holy Spirit, Giver of Life, and Blessed Virgin Mary, Star of the Sea, illuminate our journey with your light and love. As we navigate the waters of faith, guide us with your wisdom and grace, empowering us to trust deeply in God's providence.

Scripture Reading:

"But she was much perplexed by his words and pondered what sort of greeting this might be.

The angel said to her, 'Do not be afraid, Mary, for you have found favor with God.

And now, you will conceive in your womb and bear a son, and you will name him Jesus.'"

Luke 1:29-31

Reflection:

At the Annunciation, Mary faces an unimaginable call: to be the Mother of God. Her initial perplexity and fear are natural human responses to such a divine revelation. Yet, her faith and trust in God's plan overshadow her fears, marking a pivotal moment of strength and surrender. This encounter invites us to examine our own reactions to God's calls in our lives. How do we respond to the unexpected or seemingly impossible? Do we let fear and doubt dictate our actions, or do we, like Mary, place our trust in God's promise? Reflect on a time when faith guided you through uncertainty. Consider how embracing faith over fear can transform your challenges into opportunities for growth and deeper reliance on God.

Prayer of the Day:

Dear Mary, Mother of God, in your moment of doubt, you chose faith, trusting in the Lord's plan for you and all humanity. Help us to emulate your strength and faithfulness, especially when faced with the unknown. May we find courage in your example, responding to God's call with a heart full of trust and surrender. Intercede for us, that our faith may grow stronger in times of trial, and lead us closer to your Son, Jesus. Amen.

Spiritual Exercise:

Today, take a moment to meditate on the concept of faith over fear. Write down any fears currently impacting your life and prayerfully offer them to God, asking for the strength to trust in His guidance. Consider performing an act of faith, such as reaching out to someone in need or sharing a personal testimony of faith with a friend, as a tangible expression of your trust in God's plan.

Closing Prayer:

Gracious Lord, we thank You for the gift of faith and for the blessed example of the Virgin Mary, who teaches us to trust in Your ways. May her faith inspire us to walk with confidence in Your path, facing our fears with the assurance of Your loving presence. Keep us under the protective mantle of Mary, our Mother, as we seek to live our lives in faithful service to You. Amen.

Day 3

The Joy of God's Promise

Opening Prayer:

O Holy Spirit, Fountain of Living Water, and Blessed Virgin Mary, Queen of Peace, gently guide us today as we delve deeper into the mystery of God's love and promises. May your wisdom enlighten our minds and your peace fill our hearts as we journey together in prayer.

Scripture Reading:

"But Mary treasured all these words and pondered them in her heart."

Luke 2:19

Reflection:

In the quiet stillness of a stable in Bethlehem, amidst the chaos of a world unaware of the miracle that had just occurred, Mary holds onto the words of the shepherds. The scene is a tender reminder of the internal journey of faith: treasuring and pondering God's promises in our hearts. Mary's contemplative spirit invites us to reflect on how we receive and hold onto God's promises in our own lives. In moments of doubt or fear, do we recall His words with faith? How does the act of treasuring God's promises change our perspective on our circumstances? Let us take time today to ponder the promises God has made to us, allowing their truth to sink deeply into our hearts, transforming our anxiety into joy and our doubt into hope.

Prayer of the Day:

Most Holy Mary, Mother of the Word Incarnate, teach us to treasure and ponder God's promises as you did. In the quiet of our hearts, may we listen for God's voice and hold onto His words with faith and hope. Pray for us, that we might find joy and peace in believing and that our lives may be a testament to the faithfulness of God's promises. Amen.

Spiritual Exercise:

Reflect on a specific promise from Scripture that resonates with you in this season of your life. Spend some time today in quiet meditation, pondering this promise in your heart. Consider writing it down in a journal or on a piece of paper to keep as a reminder of God's faithfulness. As a practical act of faith, share this promise with someone who might need encouragement, becoming a bearer of God's joy and hope to others.

Closing Prayer:

Gracious God, we are grateful for the quiet example of Mary, who teaches us to treasure and ponder your promises. Help us to embrace your words with faith, allowing them to be a source of strength and joy in our lives. Blessed Virgin Mary, keep us steadfast in faith and joyful in hope as we walk with your Son, Jesus Christ. Amen.

Day 4

Walking in Faith with Mary

Opening Prayer:

O Holy Spirit, Source of all wisdom, and Blessed Virgin Mary, Mother of Faith, guide us on this day of our spiritual journey. Illuminate our minds and enkindle our hearts with a deepened faith and love for God. May we walk closely with you, learning from your example of unwavering trust and obedience.

Scripture Reading:

"In those days Mary set out and went with haste to a Judean town in the hill country, where she entered the house of Zechariah and greeted Elizabeth. When Elizabeth heard Mary's greeting, the child leaped in her womb. And Elizabeth was filled with the Holy Spirit and exclaimed with a loud cry:

'Blessed are you among women,

and blessed is the fruit of your womb.

And why has this happened to me,

that the mother of my Lord comes to me?

For as soon as I heard the sound of your greeting,

the child in my womb leaped for joy.

And blessed is she who believed that there would be a fulfillment of what was spoken to her by the Lord.'"

Luke 1:39-45

Reflection:

In this passage, Mary, newly bearing the Christ child within her, hurries to share her joy and the miraculous news with her cousin Elizabeth. This encounter is a beautiful illustration of faith in action—Mary's immediate response to God's call, and Elizabeth's recognition of Mary's blessedness and the presence of the Lord. This moment of shared joy and faith between two women invites us to reflect on the importance of community in our spiritual journey. How do we support and affirm God's work in each other's lives? Are we quick to share our faith and joy with those around us, encouraging and building each other up in trust and obedience to God? Let us consider how we, like Mary, can actively respond to God's call and seek to foster a community of faith that celebrates and affirms His presence in our midst.

Prayer of the Day:

Dear Mother Mary, you who journeyed in faith to share your joy and the promise of God's salvation with Elizabeth, inspire us to live with the same eagerness and faithfulness. Teach us to recognize the presence of Jesus in our lives and to share this joyous reality with others. May your example encourage us to build a supportive and faith-filled community, where the love of Christ is evident and contagious. Intercede for us, that we may always be ready to respond to God's call with a joyful "yes," just as you did. Amen.

Spiritual Exercise:

Today, reach out to someone in your faith community—perhaps a friend, family member, or fellow parishioner—and share a moment of faith or a personal testimony of how you've seen God at work in your life. This act of sharing can be a powerful means of encouragement and a way to strengthen the bonds of faith within your community. Additionally, spend some time in prayer for your faith community, asking for God's guidance and blessing upon each member as you grow together in love and obedience to His will.

Closing Prayer:

Loving God, we thank You for the gift of community and the example of faith shared between Mary and Elizabeth. Help us to cherish and foster the relationships you have placed in our lives, that we may support each other in our journey of faith. Blessed Virgin Mary, guide us in our efforts to build a community that glorifies God and serves as a of hope of His love and grace. Amen.

Day 5

The Light of God's Grace

Opening Prayer:

O Holy Spirit, Beacon of Truth, and Blessed Virgin Mary, Mirror of Justice, shine your light upon us as we continue our pilgrimage in prayer. Illuminate our path with the radiance of God's grace, guiding our steps towards deeper understanding and love.

Scripture Reading:

"On the third day, there was a wedding in Cana of Galilee, and the mother of Jesus was there. Jesus and his disciples had also been invited to the wedding. When the wine gave out, the mother of Jesus said to him, 'They have no wine.' And Jesus said to her, 'Woman, what concern is that to you and to me? My hour has not yet come.' His mother said to the servants, 'Do whatever he tells you.'"

John 2:1-5

Reflection:

At the Wedding at Cana, Mary demonstrates profound sensitivity and compassion, noticing a need before it becomes a crisis and interceding with Jesus on behalf of the hosts. Her simple, yet profound request, "They have no wine," and her directive to the servants, "Do whatever he tells you," highlight her role as an advocate and a model of faith in action. This episode invites us to reflect on the nature of intercessory prayer and the readiness to bring the needs of others before God, trusting in His providential care. It also calls us to consider our own willingness to act on God's guidance, even when the path seems unclear. How can we, like Mary, be attentive to the needs around us and trustfully bring them to Jesus? How does this story challenge us to "do whatever he tells you" in our daily lives?

Prayer of the Day:

Heavenly Mother, at Cana, you showed us the power of intercessory prayer and the importance of trusting in Jesus' word. Inspire us to follow your example, bringing the needs of our world before your Son with confidence and faith. Teach us to listen attentively for His guidance and to act with courage and trust, knowing that He can transform our scarcity into abundance. Intercede for us, that we may be bearers of God's grace, responding to His call with a willing heart. Amen.

Spiritual Exercise:

Today, identify someone in your life or in your community who is in need of prayer or assistance. Spend some time praying for this person, offering their needs to God as Mary did at Cana. Consider also a tangible way you can be of service to them, whether through a kind word, a helpful action, or a supportive presence, embodying the proactive love and concern Mary showed.

Closing Prayer:

Lord God, we thank You for the gift of Your grace, which transforms our lives and fills our emptiness with Your abundance. Through the intercession of the Blessed Virgin Mary, help us to be ever attentive to the needs of those around us, responding with the same faith and love she exemplified. Keep us under her protective mantle, that we might always seek to do Your will and be instruments of Your grace in the world. Amen.

Day 6

Trusting in God's Timing

Opening Prayer:

O Holy Spirit, Guide of all seekers, and Blessed Virgin Mary, Model of Patience, accompany us today as we seek to understand the mysteries of God's timing. Grant us the grace to trust in the divine plan, even when the path ahead seems uncertain.

Scripture Reading:

"Now every year his parents went to Jerusalem for the festival of the Passover. And when he was twelve years old, they went up as usual for the festival. When the festival was ended and they started to return, the boy Jesus stayed behind in Jerusalem, but his parents did not know it. Assuming that he was in the group of travelers, they went a day's journey. Then they started to look for him among their relatives and friends. When they did not find him, they returned to Jerusalem to search for him. After three days, they found him in the temple, sitting among the teachers, listening to them and asking them questions. And all who heard him were amazed at his understanding and his answers. When his parents saw him, they were astonished; and his mother said to him, 'Child, why have you treated us like this? Look, your father and I have been searching for you in great anxiety.' He said to them, 'Why were you searching for me? Did you not know that I must be in my Father's house?' But they did not understand what he said to them. Then he went down with them and came to Nazareth, and was obedient to them. His mother treasured all these things in her heart. And Jesus increased in wisdom and in years, and in divine and human favor."

A Pilgrimage in Prayer

Luke 2:41-52

Reflection:

This passage recounts Mary and Joseph's anxious search for Jesus, who remained in the Temple without their knowledge. Upon finding Him, Mary's response reflects a mix of relief, confusion, and faith, "Son, why have you treated us like this? Your father and I have been anxiously searching for you." Jesus' reply, "Didn't you know I had to be in my Father's house?" reveals His early awareness of His divine mission. This story invites us to ponder our own reactions to unexpected events or delays in our lives. How do we respond when God's plans diverge from our expectations? Mary's experience teaches us the virtue of trusting in God's timing, recognizing that our understanding is limited and God's wisdom is infinite. Reflect on a time when you were called to trust in God's timing. How did it challenge your faith, and what did you learn from the experience?

Prayer of the Day:

Holy Mary, Mother of God, you experienced the anxiety of a parent and the challenge of trusting in God's plans for your Son. Help us to learn from your example of patience and faith, especially when we face uncertainty or our plans are upended. Pray for us, that we may embrace God's timing with grace, trusting that He is at work in our lives, even when we do not understand His ways. Guide us to find peace in His divine will, knowing that all things work together for good for those who love God. Amen.

Spiritual Exercise:

Reflect on an area of your life where you are currently waiting or facing uncertainty. Spend some time in prayer, offering your concerns and anxieties to God, asking for the grace to trust in His timing. As a practical application, consider writing a letter to God, expressing your trust in His plan for your life, and commit to revisiting this letter in the future to see how God has worked in that situation.

Closing Prayer:

Loving Father, we thank You for the gift of Your Son, Jesus, and His Blessed Mother, Mary, who teach us the value of trusting in Your divine timing. Grant us the patience to wait on Your will and the faith to believe in Your promises, even when they are not yet visible on the horizon. Blessed Virgin Mary, keep us under your protective mantle, guiding our steps as we learn to walk in faith and trust. Amen.

Day 7

The Compassion of Mary

Opening Prayer:

O Holy Spirit, Wellspring of Love, and Blessed Virgin Mary, Refuge of Sinners, guide us today as we seek to embody the compassion and mercy that you so perfectly manifest. Open our hearts to the suffering of those around us, and inspire us to act with kindness and love.

Scripture Reading:

"And that is what the soldiers did.

Meanwhile, standing near the cross of Jesus were his mother, and his mother's sister, Mary the wife of Clopas, and Mary Magdalene. When Jesus saw his mother and the disciple whom he loved standing beside her, he said to his mother, 'Woman, here is your son.' Then he said to the disciple, 'Here is your mother.' And from that hour, the disciple took her into his own home."

John 19:25-27

Reflection:

At the foot of the cross, Mary stands as a figure of profound sorrow and compassion, witnessing the ultimate sacrifice of her son for the salvation of humanity. In this moment of intense suffering, Jesus entrusts the care of His mother to the beloved disciple, John, creating a new family bound not by blood but by love and faith. This act signifies the universal motherhood of Mary for all disciples of Christ. It prompts us to reflect on the depth of Mary's compassion, not only for her son but for all of God's children. How can we, like Mary, stand in solidarity with those who suffer in our own communities and beyond? How does this scene challenge us to accept and care for one another as members of a spiritual family?

Prayer of the Day:

Dear Mother Mary, at the foot of the cross, you showed us the depth of your compassion and the breadth of your motherly love. Help us to learn from your example, to stand beside those who suffer, and to see Christ in everyone we meet. Grant us the courage to act as your son commanded, taking care of one another with the love and compassion you exemplify. Intercede for us, that we may be filled with the strength and grace to embrace all God's children as our brothers and sisters. Amen.

Spiritual Exercise:

Today, identify someone in your life or community who is experiencing suffering or hardship. Consider how you might offer them support or companionship, following Mary's example of compassionate presence. This could be through a listening ear, a comforting word, or a practical act of assistance. Reflect on how this action not only aids the one who suffers but also draws you closer to living out the Christian call to love and compassion.

Closing Prayer:

Gracious God, we thank You for the gift of Your mother, Mary, who stands as a beacon of compassion and love in the face of suffering. Through her intercession, help us to open our hearts to the needs of others, sharing in their sorrows and joys as if they were our own. Blessed Virgin Mary, keep us under your protective mantle, guiding us to live out our call to be instruments of Your love and mercy in the world. Amen.

Day 8

Mary's Role as Intercessor

Opening Prayer:

O Holy Spirit, Giver of Grace, and Blessed Virgin Mary, Advocate for your children, guide us today as we seek to understand and appreciate the depth of your intercessory role in our lives. Help us to draw nearer to you, confident in your maternal care and advocacy.

Scripture Reading:

"In the sixth month, the angel Gabriel was sent by God to a town in Galilee called Nazareth, to a virgin engaged to a man whose name was Joseph, of the house of David. The virgin's name was Mary. And he came to her and said, 'Greetings, favored one! The Lord is with you.' But she was much perplexed by his words and pondered what sort of greeting this might be. The angel said to her, 'Do not be afraid, Mary, for you have found favor with God. And now, you will conceive in your womb and bear a son, and you will name him Jesus. He will be great and will be called the Son of the Most High, and the Lord God will give to him the throne of his ancestor David. He will reign over the house of Jacob forever, and of his kingdom, there will be no end.'

Mary said to the angel, 'How can this be, since I am a virgin?' The angel said to her, 'The Holy Spirit will come upon you, and the power of the Most High will overshadow you; therefore, the child to be born will be holy; he will be called the Son of God. And now, your relative Elizabeth in her old age has also conceived a son; and this is the sixth month for her who was said to be barren. For nothing will be impossible with God.'

Then Mary said, 'Here am I, the servant of the Lord; let it be with me according to your word.' Then the angel departed from her."

Luke 1:26-38

Reflection:

The Annunciation marks a pivotal moment in salvation history, where Mary's 'yes' to God's plan paves the way for the coming of Christ into the world. This encounter between Mary and the angel Gabriel reveals Mary not only as the Mother of God but also as an intercessor, whose willingness to accept God's will brings divine grace into the world. Mary's response, "Behold, I am the handmaid of the Lord; let it be to me according to your word," reflects her deep faith and her role as a mediator of God's grace. This passage invites us to reflect on Mary's intercessory power, asking for her prayers and guidance in our own lives. How can Mary's example inspire us to be open to God's will? In what ways might we seek Mary's intercession for our own needs and the needs of the world?

Prayer of the Day:

Most Holy Mary, Mother of God and our mother, you answered God's call with faith and humility, becoming the vessel through which salvation entered the world. Teach us to trust in your intercessory power and to turn to you in our needs. As you interceded at Cana, intercede for us now, bringing our prayers before your Son with the same love and concern you showed during your earthly life. Help us to be open to God's will, following your example of faithful service and devotion. Amen.

Spiritual Exercise:

Today, take a moment to entrust a particular intention or need to Mary, asking for her intercession with confidence and faith. This can be a personal need, a concern for a loved one, or a prayer for the world. Consider writing your intention down and placing it in a spot where you will be reminded to ask for Mary's intercession regularly. Additionally, reflect on how you can serve as an intercessor for others, offering prayers and support to those in need as Mary does for us.

Closing Prayer:

Lord God, we thank you for the gift of Mary, our Advocate and Helper. Through her intercession, may we receive the grace we need to navigate the challenges of life. Strengthen our faith and our commitment to your will, that we might live as true disciples of your Son. Blessed Virgin Mary, keep us in your prayers, guiding us ever closer to Jesus, our saviour and Redeemer. Amen.

Day 9

Embracing God's Peace Through Mary

Opening Prayer:

O Holy Spirit, Prince of Peace, and Blessed Virgin Mary, Queen of Peace, guide us on this day as we seek to embody the tranquility and serenity you so perfectly model. Teach us to find God's peace in the midst of our daily challenges and to become instruments of that peace in our world.

Scripture Reading:

"While they were there, the time came for her to deliver her child. And she gave birth to her firstborn son and wrapped him in bands of cloth, and laid him in a manger, because there was no place for them in the inn."

Luke 2:6-7

Reflection:

In the simplicity and quiet of a stable, Mary gave birth to Jesus, the Prince of Peace. This humble setting underscores the profound truth that God's peace often enters the world not with grandeur but in quiet, unexpected places. Mary's calm trust in God's provision, even in less-than-ideal circumstances, serves as a powerful example for us. It invites us to consider where we are seeking peace in our own lives and to remember that true peace comes from God and is often found in simplicity and surrender to His will. How can we, like Mary, create space in our hearts and lives for God's peace? In what ways can we offer this peace to others, especially in situations of conflict or difficulty?

Prayer of the Day:

Holy Mary, Mother of the Prince of Peace, in the silence of the stable, you welcomed Jesus into the world, embodying the deep peace that comes from God. Intercede for us, that we may find this peace in our own hearts, amidst the noise and haste of our lives. Help us to trust in God's loving plan for us, as you did, and to extend His peace to everyone we encounter. May our lives reflect the peace of Christ, bringing light and hope to those in darkness. Amen.

Spiritual Exercise:

Today, take a few moments to meditate on the concept of peace. Consider starting or ending your day with a quiet moment of reflection, asking God to fill you with His peace. Identify one action you can take to be a peacemaker in your own environment—this could be as simple as offering a kind word, listening to someone in need, or resolving a small conflict with compassion and understanding. Reflect on how embracing God's peace can transform not only your heart but also the world around you.

Closing Prayer:

Lord God, we thank You for the gift of Your peace, embodied so perfectly in Mary and her Son, Jesus. Grant us the grace to seek and find Your peace in every aspect of our lives, and the strength to be peacemakers in our world. May the example of Mary inspire us to trust in You and to spread Your peace wherever we go. Blessed Virgin Mary, keep us safe under your protective mantle, always leading us closer to your Son, the source of all peace. Amen.

Day 10

Mary's Faithfulness Through Trials

Opening Prayer:

O Holy Spirit, Source of Strength, and Blessed Virgin Mary, Model of Faithful Endurance, guide us today as we seek to understand the depth of your perseverance and trust in God through the trials of life. Strengthen our resolve and deepen our faith as we walk in your footsteps.

Scripture Reading:

"And that is what the soldiers did.

Meanwhile, standing near the cross of Jesus were his mother, and his mother's sister, Mary the wife of Clopas, and Mary Magdalene. When Jesus saw his mother and the disciple whom he loved standing beside her, he said to his mother, 'Woman, here is your son.' Then he said to the disciple, 'Here is your mother.' And from that hour, the disciple took her into his own home."

John 19:25-27

Reflection:

At the foot of the cross, Mary stands as a testament to unwavering faith and steadfast love in the face of unimaginable sorrow. Her presence during Jesus' crucifixion highlights her role as a witness to the fulfillment of God's promise, even as it pierces her heart with grief. This moment invites us to reflect on the nature of faithfulness, especially during life's most challenging trials. Mary's example teaches us that faithfulness does not mean an absence of pain or doubt but a continued trust and presence in God's plan, despite the darkness. How does Mary's endurance inspire you in your own struggles? How can her faithfulness encourage you to remain close to Jesus, especially when the path is marked by suffering?

Prayer of the Day:

Holy Mary, Mother of Sorrows, you stood by your Son in His darkest hour with courage and faith. In your suffering, you embraced God's will with a heart both grieving and trusting. Pray for us, that we may have the strength to face our trials with the same faithfulness and love. Help us to stand firm in faith, even when hope seems distant, trusting that God's love will prevail. May we, like you, remain close to Jesus in all the seasons of our life, confident in the victory of His resurrection. Amen.

Spiritual Exercise:

Reflect on a current challenge or trial in your life. Spend some time in prayer, offering this situation to God and asking for Mary's intercession to endure this trial with faith and hope. Consider performing an act of devotion in honour of Mary's faithfulness, such as praying the Rosary or reading a passage from Scripture that speaks of God's faithfulness in times of trouble. Let this act be a reminder of your desire to remain faithful and close to God, no matter the circumstances.

Closing Prayer:

Gracious God, we thank You for the gift of Mary, our Mother, who teaches us the meaning of faithfulness in suffering. Through her intercession, grant us the grace to bear our crosses with love, to stand by Jesus in His suffering, and to trust in Your redeeming love. May our lives be a testament to the faith that withstands trials, rooted in the hope of Christ's resurrection. Blessed Virgin Mary, guide us with your gentle strength, leading us ever closer to your Son, our saviour. Amen.

Day 11

Mary's Quiet Contemplation

Opening Prayer:

O Holy Spirit, Whisper of Wisdom, and Blessed Virgin Mary, Seat of Wisdom, guide us into the depths of contemplation and understanding on this day. Help us to quiet our minds and open our hearts to the insights and inspirations you wish to impart.

Scripture Reading:

"But Mary treasured all these words and pondered them in her heart."

Luke 2:19

Reflection:

In the bustling narrative of Christ's Nativity, this verse stands as a serene pool of reflection. Mary, amidst the wonder and chaos of the birth of Jesus, treasures and ponders the events deeply within her heart. This moment of introspection and contemplation reveals Mary's profound connection with God and her role as a model for contemplative prayer. Her example invites us to find moments of quiet reflection in our own lives, to treasure and ponder the workings of God in our midst. How often do we take the time to quietly reflect on our experiences, seeing them through the lens of faith? How can Mary's example of contemplation lead us to a deeper understanding of God's presence in our lives and the world?

Prayer of the Day:

Blessed Virgin Mary, in the silence of your heart, you contemplated the great mysteries of our salvation. Teach us to seek moments of quiet reflection, that we might treasure and ponder the workings of God in our lives. Help us to cultivate a contemplative heart, one that sees beyond the surface of our daily experiences to the profound depths of God's love and wisdom. May our contemplation bring us closer to your Son, Jesus, the source of all wisdom and peace. Amen.

Spiritual Exercise:

Set aside some time today for quiet contemplation. Choose a passage from Scripture, a facet of Mary's life, or an aspect of your own life journey. Reflect on this quietly, asking for the grace to see with the eyes of faith. Consider keeping a journal to record insights and inspirations received during this time of reflection. Let this practice be a step towards making contemplative prayer a regular part of your spiritual journey, following the example of Mary.

Closing Prayer:

Lord God, we thank You for the gift of Mary, our model of contemplation and reflection. Through her intercession, help us to cultivate quiet spaces in our lives for prayer and meditation. Grant us the grace to treasure and ponder Your presence and action in our lives, that we might grow in wisdom, love, and understanding. May our hearts always be attuned to the whisper of Your Spirit, guiding us closer to You through Mary's example. Amen.

Day 12

Mary as the First Disciple

Opening Prayer:

O Holy Spirit, Guide on our journey, and Blessed Virgin Mary, first among disciples, lead us today as we seek to follow in your footsteps. Enlighten our path with the lessons of your discipleship, that we may walk it with faith and devotion.

Scripture Reading

"Then Mary said, 'Here am I, the servant of the Lord; let it be with me according to your word.' Then the angel departed from her."

Luke 1:38

Reflection:

In this moment of profound submission to God's will, Mary exemplifies what it means to be a true disciple. Her response to the angel Gabriel's announcement is not just acceptance but a wholehearted embrace of God's plan, despite the uncertainties and challenges it would bring. This pivotal moment in salvation history showcases Mary's faith, courage, and willingness to serve, characteristics that define her as the first and model disciple of Christ. Her example prompts us to consider the depth of our own discipleship. Are we, like Mary, ready to say, "Let it be with me according to your word"? How does Mary's example challenge and inspire us to live out our calling as disciples of Christ in our daily lives?

Prayer of the Day:

Dear Mary, Mother of God and our mother, your fiat marks the beginning of your journey as the first disciple of Jesus. Inspire us with your example of faith and obedience to God's will. Help us to live out our discipleship with the same courage and zeal that you showed, always ready to serve the Lord and His people. Intercede for us, that we may have the grace to follow Jesus more closely, carrying our crosses with love and trust in God's providential care. Amen.

Spiritual Exercise:

Reflect on your own journey of discipleship. Identify one area in your life where you feel called to deepen your commitment to following Christ. It might be through greater service to others, more dedicated prayer time, or a more courageous witness to your faith. Commit to one concrete action this week that reflects your desire to follow Jesus more closely, inspired by Mary's example of discipleship. Consider sharing this commitment with a friend or family member for accountability and support.

Closing Prayer:

Lord Jesus, we thank you for giving us Mary, your mother, as the model of perfect discipleship. Through her intercession, help us to grow in our love for you and in our dedication to your mission. May our lives reflect her fiat, as we seek to do your will with joy and humility. Blessed Virgin Mary, keep guiding us on our journey of faith, leading us ever closer to your Son. Amen.

A Pilgrimage in Prayer

Day 13

Mary's Journey of Faith

Opening Prayer:

O Holy Spirit, Guide of the faithful, and Blessed Virgin Mary, Beacon of Trust, accompany us on our journey today as we seek to deepen our understanding of faith through your example. Enlighten our minds and strengthen our hearts to follow God's path with unwavering trust.

Scripture Reading:

"Now every year his parents went to Jerusalem for the festival of the Passover. And when he was twelve years old, they went up as usual for the festival. When the festival was ended and they started to return, the boy Jesus stayed behind in Jerusalem, but his parents did not know it. Assuming that he was in the group of travelers, they went a day's journey. Then they started to look for him among their relatives and friends. When they did not find him, they returned to Jerusalem to search for him. After three days they found him in the temple, sitting among the teachers, listening to them and asking them questions. And all who heard him were amazed at his understanding and his answers. When his parents saw him, they were astonished; and his mother said to him, 'Child, why have you treated us like this? Look, your father and I have been searching for you in great anxiety.' He said to them, 'Why were you searching for me? Did you not know that I must be in my Father's house?' But they did not understand what he said to them. Then he went down with them and came to Nazareth, and was obedient to them. His mother treasured all these things in her heart. And Jesus increased in wisdom and in years, and in divine and human favor."

William Gomes

Luke 2:41-52

Reflection:

Mary's journey of faith was not without its moments of uncertainty and anxiety, as evidenced by the episode of the finding in the Temple. When Jesus lingers in Jerusalem without Mary and Joseph's knowledge, they experience the distress any parent would feel upon losing a child. Mary's response to Jesus, upon finding Him, "Son, why have you treated us so? Your father and I have been searching for you in great anxiety," reveals her human vulnerability. Yet, even in this moment of parental worry, Mary's faith remains intact. She listens to Jesus' explanation, pondering these events in her heart, allowing her faith to grow through the experience. This narrative invites us to reflect on our own responses to the unforeseen trials of life. How do we react when faced with situations that test our faith? Can we, like Mary, remain open to the lessons these challenges teach us about trust, patience, and surrender to God's will?

Prayer of the Day:

Blessed Virgin Mary, throughout your life, you faced moments of joy and uncertainty with a steadfast faith. In your anxiety and search for Jesus, you teach us the importance of trust in God's plan. Help us to learn from your example, to search for Jesus in all things, and to keep our hearts open to the lessons of faith He teaches us along the way. Intercede for us, that our faith may be strengthened in times of doubt and that we may always turn to you as our model of faithful perseverance. Amen.

Spiritual Exercise:

Today, reflect on a recent challenge or trial that has tested your faith. Spend some time in prayer, asking for Mary's intercession to help you see where Jesus is leading you through this experience. Consider journaling about the situation, focusing on what you have learned or can learn about trust, patience, and surrender. As a practical action, reach out to someone who is currently experiencing their own trial of faith and offer them support and encouragement, sharing the comfort and guidance you have received through your own reflection and prayer.

Closing Prayer:

Lord God, we thank You for the Blessed Virgin Mary, who teaches us by her example how to live a life of faith, even in the face of uncertainty and trial. Through her intercession, grant us the grace to grow in faith and trust in You, no matter the challenges we face. May our lives reflect the depth of our faith and our commitment to following You, guided by Mary, our mother and model. Amen.

Day 14

Mary's Heart of Service

Opening Prayer:

O Holy Spirit, Fountain of Charity, and Blessed Virgin Mary, Exemplar of Service, guide us today as we seek to emulate your loving service in our lives. Illuminate our path with the light of compassion and charity, that we may follow in your footsteps.

Scripture Reading:

"On the third day, there was a wedding in Cana of Galilee, and the mother of Jesus was there. Jesus and his disciples had also been invited to the wedding. When the wine gave out, the mother of Jesus said to him, 'They have no wine.' And Jesus said to her, 'Woman, what concern is that to you and to me? My hour has not yet come.' His mother said to the servants, 'Do whatever he tells you.'

Now standing there were six stone water jars for the Jewish rites of purification, each holding twenty or thirty gallons. Jesus said to them, 'Fill the jars with water.' And they filled them up to the brim. He said to them, 'Now draw some out, and take it to the chief steward.' So they took it. When the steward tasted the water that had become wine, and did not know where it came from (though the servants who had drawn the water knew), the steward called the bridegroom and said to him, 'Everyone serves the good wine first, and then the inferior wine after the guests have become drunk. But you have kept the good wine until now.' Jesus did this, the first of his signs, in Cana of Galilee, and revealed his glory; and his disciples believed in him."

John 2:1-11

Reflection:

The Wedding at Cana presents Mary not only as a concerned mother but also as a model of attentive service. Her observance of the wine running out and her prompt intercession with Jesus demonstrate her profound sensitivity to the needs of others. Mary's actions at Cana teach us the importance of service born out of genuine love and concern. She instructs the servants, "Do whatever he tells you," guiding them towards trust in Jesus' words. This narrative invites us to reflect on our own willingness to serve those around us and to intercede on their behalf. How does Mary's example inspire us to be more attentive to the needs of our community? How can we, through our actions and prayers, bring the transformative presence of Jesus into the lives of those we serve?

Prayer of the Day:

Dear Mary, Mother of Divine Grace, at Cana, you showed us the power of compassionate service and the importance of turning to Jesus in every need. Inspire us to follow your example, to be attentive to the needs of those around us, and to serve with a heart full of love and humility. Teach us to trust in Jesus' words and to bring His miraculous grace into the ordinary circumstances of our daily lives. Intercede for us, that our lives may be a testament to the joy and fulfillment found in serving others in the name of your Son. Amen.

Spiritual Exercise:

Identify a need within your family, community, or place of work where you can offer your service today. It could be as simple as lending an ear to someone who needs to talk, offering your help to someone struggling with a task, or performing an act of kindness for a stranger. Let your service be a silent prayer, an offering to God through the hands of Mary. Reflect on how this act of service makes you feel and how it impacts the person or people you are helping. Consider making a habit of identifying and responding to a call for service each day, as a way of living out your devotion to Mary and her Son.

Closing Prayer:

We thank You, Lord, for the blessed example of Mary, who teaches us the value and beauty of serving others with love and dedication. May her intercession strengthen us as we strive to live out our call to service, bringing Your love and compassion to all we meet. Keep us under the protective mantle of Mary, our Mother, guiding us ever closer to You through acts of kindness and service. Amen.

A Pilgrimage in Prayer

Day 15

Finding Strength in Mary's Faith

Opening Prayer:

O Holy Spirit, Source of all courage, and Blessed Virgin Mary, Pillar of Faith, guide us on this day as we seek to draw strength from your unwavering faith in God's promises. Enlighten us with your wisdom and fortify our hearts with the courage to face our own challenges.

Scripture Reading:

"Now after they had left, an angel of the Lord appeared to Joseph in a dream and said, 'Get up, take the child and his mother, and flee to Egypt, and remain there until I tell you; for Herod is about to search for the child, to destroy him.' Then Joseph got up, took the child and his mother by night, and went to Egypt, and remained there until the death of Herod. This was to fulfill what had been spoken by the Lord through the prophet, 'Out of Egypt I have called my son.'"

Matthew 2:13-15

Reflection:

In the dead of night, Mary and Joseph flee to Egypt with the infant Jesus, escaping Herod's wrath. This moment of crisis reveals Mary's strength and trust in God's protection over her family. Amidst uncertainty and danger, Mary's faith does not waver; she embarks on a journey into the unknown, trusting in God's guidance and provision. This episode invites us to reflect on our own responses to the crises and challenges in our lives. Like Mary, are we able to trust in God's promises and face our fears with faith? How can Mary's example of strength and trust in the midst of adversity inspire us to lean not on our understanding but on God's unfailing love and protection?

Prayer of the Day:

Blessed Virgin Mary, in your flight into Egypt, you showed us the meaning of trust and strength in the face of danger and uncertainty. Help us to emulate your unwavering faith in God's promise of protection and guidance. Intercede for us, that we may face the challenges and fears in our lives with the same courage and trust in the Lord. May we, like you, find our strength in faith, knowing that God is with us in every moment of trial and transition. Amen.

Spiritual Exercise:

Consider a current situation in your life that is causing you fear or uncertainty. Spend some time in prayer, offering this situation to God and asking for Mary's intercession to help you navigate it with faith and courage. As a practical action, write down the fears you are facing and next to each one, write a promise from Scripture that speaks of God's protection, guidance, or faithfulness. Keep this list as a reminder of God's presence and Mary's example of faith in your life.

Closing Prayer:

Lord God, we thank you for the Blessed Virgin Mary, whose faith and trust in Your divine will serves as a beacon of light for us in times of darkness. Through her intercession, grant us the grace to face our fears with courage, to trust in Your guidance, and to find strength in the knowledge of Your love and protection. May our lives be a testament to the power of faith, inspired by Mary, our mother and guide. Amen.

A Pilgrimage in Prayer

Day 16

Mary's Example of Listening

Opening Prayer:

O Holy Spirit, Voice of Truth, and Blessed Virgin Mary, Model of Attentive Listening, open our hearts today as we seek to hear God's voice in our lives. Guide us in our quest for understanding, and help us to be responsive to the whispers of your wisdom.

Scripture Reading:

"Now as they went on their way, he entered a certain village, where a woman named Martha welcomed him into her home. She had a sister named Mary, who sat at the Lord's feet and listened to what he was saying. But Martha was distracted by her many tasks; so she came to him and asked, 'Lord, do you not care that my sister has left me to do all the work by myself? Tell her then to help me.' But the Lord answered her, 'Martha, Martha, you are worried and distracted by many things; there is need of only one thing. Mary has chosen the better part, which will not be taken away from her.'"

Luke 10:38

Reflection:

Though traditionally associated with Mary of Nazareth, the story of Mary and Martha offers a valuable lesson on the importance of listening—a virtue exemplified by the Mother of God throughout her life. In this passage, Mary chooses to sit at Jesus' feet, listening to His teaching, while Martha is preoccupied with the duties of hospitality. Jesus affirms Mary's choice, emphasizing the value of being present and attentive to His words. This narrative invites us to consider our own tendencies to be either like Martha, caught up in the busyness of life, or like Mary, focused on the essential aspect of listening to the Lord. How often do we allow the noise of our daily responsibilities to drown out God's voice? How can we cultivate a more attentive heart, following the example of Mary, who pondered God's word and presence in her life?

Prayer of the Day:

Dear Blessed Virgin Mary, you who listened to God's word with a heart full of faith and love, teach us to quiet our minds and open our hearts to listen to Him. Help us to discern what is truly important and to choose the better part, as you did throughout your life. Pray for us, that we may find the space and silence necessary to encounter God in the depths of our being, transforming our lives with His grace. Amen.

Spiritual Exercise:

Today, take a moment to practice the art of spiritual listening. Find a quiet place where you can be free from distractions. Read a passage from Scripture slowly, paying attention to any word or phrase that stands out to you. Reflect on what God might be saying to you through this passage. Consider journaling your thoughts and prayers, or simply sitting in silence, allowing God's voice to resonate in your heart. As you go about your day, remain open to the ways God continues to speak to you through the people and situations you encounter.

Closing Prayer:

We thank you, Lord, for the gift of your word and the example of the Blessed Virgin Mary, who teaches us the importance of listening to your voice. Grant us the grace to prioritize time with you, to listen deeply, and to respond with love. May Mary's example inspire us to seek you in all things and to live according to your will. Blessed Virgin Mary, keep us under your protective mantle, always drawing us closer to your Son, Jesus. Amen.

Day 17

Mary's Witness to Joy

Opening Prayer:

O Holy Spirit, Bringer of Joy, and Blessed Virgin Mary, Cause of our Joy, guide us on this day to discover the profound joy found in living according to God's will. Help us to embrace the happiness that comes from serving the Lord with a whole heart.

Scripture Reading:

"In those days Mary set out and went with haste to a Judean town in the hill country, where she entered the house of Zechariah and greeted Elizabeth. When Elizabeth heard Mary's greeting, the child leaped in her womb. And Elizabeth was filled with the Holy Spirit and exclaimed with a loud cry:

'Blessed are you among women,

and blessed is the fruit of your womb.

And why has this happened to me,

that the mother of my Lord comes to me?

For as soon as I heard the sound of your greeting,

the child in my womb leaped for joy.

And blessed is she who believed that there would be a fulfillment of what was spoken to her by the Lord.'"

Luke 1:39-45

Reflection:

In the visitation, Mary, newly pregnant with Jesus, hurries to share her joy and the miraculous news with her cousin Elizabeth. This encounter is a beautiful testament to the joy that comes from God's presence within us and among us. Elizabeth's greeting, "Blessed are you among women, and blessed is the fruit of your womb," and her declaration that "the child in my womb leaped for joy" at the sound of Mary's voice, highlight the deep, spiritual joy that accompanies the fulfillment of God's promises. This passage invites us to reflect on our own experiences of joy in God's presence and the ways in which we share this joy with others. How does Mary's example inspire us to seek and celebrate the joy of the Lord in our lives? How can we, like Mary, be bearers of joy to those we encounter?

Prayer of the Day:

Dear Mary, Mother of Joy, your visit to Elizabeth spread the joy of the Lord and made manifest His presence in the world. Pray for us, that we may also be carriers of this divine joy, sharing it generously with our families, friends, and all whom we meet. Help us to recognize and rejoice in the everyday miracles that testify to God's love and grace in our lives. May our hearts always leap for joy in the Lord, as we live in gratitude for His countless blessings. Amen.

Spiritual Exercise:

Today, reflect on a recent moment when you experienced God's joy in your life. It could be a moment of prayer, an encounter with another person, or a time when you witnessed beauty in creation. Consider sharing this experience with someone as a way of spreading God's joy. Alternatively, engage in an activity that brings you joy and offer it as a prayer of thanksgiving to God. Let this action be a reminder of the joy that comes from living in communion with Him and with others.

Closing Prayer:

We thank You, Lord, for the gift of joy that permeates our lives, a joy that has its source in Your love and fidelity. Through the intercession of the Blessed Virgin Mary, help us to live as joyful witnesses to Your grace, spreading your cheer and hope wherever we go. May our lives reflect the happiness that comes from serving You, drawing others closer to Your merciful heart. Blessed Virgin Mary, keep us under your protective mantle, always leading us closer to the source of all joy, Jesus Christ our Lord. Amen.

Day 18

Emulating Mary's Patience

Opening Prayer:

O Holy Spirit, Teacher of patience, and Blessed Virgin Mary, Example of serene trust, guide our hearts today as we seek to learn from your example of patient endurance and steadfast faith. Help us to cultivate a spirit of patience in our journey with God and with each other.

Scripture Reading:

"When the time came for their purification according to the law of Moses, they brought him up to Jerusalem to present him to the Lord (as it is written in the law of the Lord, 'Every firstborn male shall be designated as holy to the Lord'), and they offered a sacrifice according to what is stated in the law of the Lord, 'a pair of turtledoves or two young pigeons.'

Now there was a man in Jerusalem whose name was Simeon; this man was righteous and devout, looking forward to the consolation of Israel, and the Holy Spirit rested on him. It had been revealed to him by the Holy Spirit that he would not see death before he had seen the Lord's Messiah. Guided by the Spirit, Simeon came into the temple; and when the parents brought in the child Jesus, to do for him what was customary under the law, Simeon took him in his arms and praised God, saying:

'Master, now you are dismissing your servant in peace,

according to your word;

for my eyes have seen your salvation,

which you have prepared in the presence of all peoples,

a light for revelation to the Gentiles

and for glory to your people Israel.'

And the child's father and mother were amazed at what was being said about him. Then Simeon blessed them and said to his mother Mary, 'This child is destined for the falling and the rising of many in Israel, and to be a sign that will be opposed so that the inner thoughts of many will be revealed—and a sword will pierce your own soul too.'"

Luke 2:22-35

Reflection:

The Presentation of Jesus in the Temple not only fulfills the Jewish law but also reveals the depth of Mary's patience and faith in God's promises. Simeon's prophecy to Mary, that a sword would pierce her own soul, foreshadows the future sorrows she would endure as the mother of Jesus. This moment highlights Mary's role in the salvation narrative—not just as the mother of Christ but as a participant in the redemptive suffering of her son. Mary's acceptance of Simeon's words reflects her profound patience and trust in God's plan, even when it promises hardship. This passage invites us to reflect on our own patience in the face of uncertainty and suffering. How do we respond to the trials and delays in our lives? Can we, like Mary, trust in God's timing and plan, even when the road ahead seems fraught with difficulty?

Prayer of the Day:

Dear Mary, Mother of Sorrows, your patience and trust in the face of prophecy and pain inspire us to bear our own crosses with grace. Teach us to embrace God's will with open hearts, trusting in His wisdom and timing, even when His plans challenge us. Help us to endure our trials with patience, knowing that, like you, we are never alone in our suffering. Intercede for us, that we may find strength in faith and hope in the promises of God. Amen.

Spiritual Exercise:

Today, identify an area in your life where you are struggling with impatience or facing a trial that tests your endurance. Spend some time in prayer, offering this situation to God and asking for the grace to wait patiently for His guidance and resolution. Consider writing a letter to Mary, expressing your struggles and asking for her intercession in cultivating patience and trust in God's plan. As a practical action, practice a small act of patience today, whether it's in a conversation, while completing a task, or in a moment of waiting, as a tangible reminder of your desire to grow in this virtue.

Closing Prayer:

We thank You, Lord, for the gift of Mary, our mother, who teaches us the value of patience and trust in Your divine plan. Through her intercession, grant us the strength to face our trials with courage and grace, knowing that in every moment of waiting, You are with us. May our lives reflect the patience and faith of Mary, as we walk in trust and hope towards the fulfillment of Your promises. Amen.

Day 19

Mary's Role as a Mother to All

Opening Prayer:

O Holy Spirit, Giver of Life, and Blessed Virgin Mary, Mother to us all, guide our hearts today as we reflect on the depth of your maternal love and care for humanity. Enrich our understanding and appreciation for your gentle guidance in our journey towards holiness.

Scripture Reading:

"When Jesus saw his mother and the disciple whom he loved standing beside her, he said to his mother, 'Woman, here is your son.' Then he said to the disciple, 'Here is your mother.' And from that hour the disciple took her into his own home."

John 19:26-27

Reflection:

In the midst of His agony on the cross, Jesus entrusts Mary to John, symbolically establishing her as the mother of all disciples. This poignant moment not only highlights the personal relationship between Mary and the Church but also underscores her role in our spiritual lives as a nurturing, guiding, and interceding presence. Mary's acceptance of this role exemplifies her unconditional love and willingness to embrace all of God's children as her own. This act invites us to consider how we relate to Mary as our spiritual mother. Do we turn to her in our times of need, seeking her guidance and intercession? How can we cultivate a deeper relationship with Mary, allowing her to lead us closer to Christ?

Prayer of the Day:

Blessed Virgin Mary, Mother of the Church and our mother, your acceptance at the foot of the cross has opened the way for us to come to you in our needs, joys, and sorrows. Teach us to embrace your loving care and to seek your guidance in our journey of faith. Intercede for us with your Son, that we may experience the fullness of His love and mercy. Help us to open our hearts to your maternal guidance, that we may grow in holiness and in love for Jesus, our Savior. Amen.

Spiritual Exercise:

Reflect on your relationship with Mary as your spiritual mother. Consider setting aside time today for a Marian devotion, such as the Rosary, the Angelus, or a simple prayer of consecration to Mary. As you engage in this devotion, express your desires, worries, and hopes to Mary, trusting in her maternal intercession. Contemplate how you can honor Mary in your daily life, perhaps by emulating her virtues or by fostering devotion to her in your family or community.

Closing Prayer:

We thank You, Lord, for the gift of Mary, our mother, who stands beside us in every moment of our lives. Through her intercession, may we draw ever closer to you, growing in love and in grace. May Mary's example inspire us to live our lives in service to others, reflecting the love and compassion of Christ. Keep us under the protective mantle of Mary, guiding us safely on our path to eternal life with you. Amen.

Day 20

Mary's Solace in Sorrow

Opening Prayer:

O Holy Spirit, Comforter of the afflicted, and Blessed Virgin Mary, Refuge in times of sorrow, guide us today as we seek to find peace and solace in the midst of our trials. Teach us to turn to you in our moments of pain, trusting in your compassionate embrace.

Scripture Reading:

"And that is what the soldiers did. Meanwhile, standing near the cross of Jesus were his mother, and his mother's sister, Mary the wife of Clopas, and Mary Magdalene. When Jesus saw his mother and the disciple whom he loved standing beside her, he said to his mother, 'Woman, here is your son.' Then he said to the disciple, 'Here is your mother.' And from that hour the disciple took her into his own home."

John 19:25-27

Reflection:

At the foot of the cross, Mary stands as a profound witness to faithfulness and strength in the face of unimaginable sorrow. Her presence during Jesus' crucifixion embodies the depth of a mother's love and the anguish of watching a child suffer. This moment in Mary's life invites us to reflect on the nature of solace and comfort in times of grief. Mary's unwavering faith and her ability to stand firm in the face of her Son's suffering offer us a model for handling our own sorrows. How do we seek comfort in our moments of pain? Can we, like Mary, find strength in our faith and the community that surrounds us? Mary's example teaches us that even in the darkest moments, we are not alone—God's love and Mary's maternal care are with us, offering solace and hope.

Prayer of the Day:

Blessed Virgin Mary, Mother of Sorrows, in your darkest hour, you remained close to Jesus, drawing strength from your faith. Help us to learn from your example, to face our sorrows with courage and to find comfort in the knowledge that we are never alone. Intercede for us in our times of need, bringing our prayers before your Son, that we may receive the grace to endure and the hope to see beyond our grief. May your tender love guide us towards peace and healing. Amen.

Spiritual Exercise:

Today, take a moment to reflect on a recent sorrow or difficulty in your life. Light a candle as a symbol of Christ's presence in your darkness. Spend some time in prayer, offering your pain to Jesus and asking Mary to comfort and accompany you in your suffering. Consider writing a letter to Mary, expressing your feelings and asking for her maternal intercession. As a practical act of faith, reach out to someone who is also experiencing sorrow, offering them words of comfort or a listening ear, as a way to embody Mary's compassion and care.

Closing Prayer:

Lord God, we thank You for the gift of Mary, who knew the depths of human sorrow and yet remained steadfast in her faith. Through her intercession, grant us the grace to endure our trials with hope, finding solace in Your love and comfort in the community of believers. May we, inspired by Mary's example, become sources of comfort and hope to others in their times of need. Amen.

Day 21

Mary as a Beacon of Hope

Opening Prayer:

O Holy Spirit, Source of all hope, and Blessed Virgin Mary, Star of Hope, illuminate our journey today as we seek to draw strength from your unwavering trust in God's promises. Enkindle in us a flame of hope that no hardship can extinguish.

Scripture Reading:

"Now there was a man in Jerusalem whose name was Simeon; this man was righteous and devout, looking forward to the consolation of Israel, and the Holy Spirit rested on him. It had been revealed to him by the Holy Spirit that he would not see death before he had seen the Lord's Messiah. Guided by the Spirit, Simeon came into the temple; and when the parents brought in the child Jesus, to do for him what was customary under the law, Simeon took him in his arms and praised God, saying:

'Master, now you are dismissing your servant in peace,

according to your word;

for my eyes have seen your salvation,

which you have prepared in the presence of all peoples,

a light for revelation to the Gentiles

and for glory to your people Israel.'

And the child's father and mother were amazed at what was being said about him. Then Simeon blessed them and said to his mother Mary, 'This child is destined for the falling and the rising of many in Israel, and to be a sign that will be opposed so that the inner thoughts of many will be revealed—and a sword will pierce your own soul too.'"

Luke 2:25-35

Reflection:

In the temple, Mary encounters Simeon, who, moved by the Holy Spirit, prophesies the pivotal role Jesus will play in the salvation of humanity and the sorrow that will pierce Mary's own soul. This moment is a profound blend of promise and pain, highlighting Mary's strength and hope amidst foretold suffering. Mary's journey reflects the essence of hope — a steadfast belief in God's goodness and faithfulness, even when faced with the certainty of trials. This encounter invites us to reflect on our understanding of hope. How does Mary's acceptance of both the promise and the prophecy deepen our own sense of hope in God's plan? In what ways does hope sustain us through our trials, as it did for Mary?

Prayer of the Day:

Dear Mary, Mother of Hope, in the face of Simeon's prophecy, you embraced your role in God's plan with courage and trust. Help us to follow your example, to live with hope that does not falter in the face of life's trials. Intercede for us, that our hearts may be anchored in the hope of Christ, finding peace and strength in the promise of salvation. May we, like you, navigate the challenges of life with a spirit of trust and hopefulness, always looking to the light of Christ to guide our way. Amen.

Spiritual Exercise:

Reflect on a situation in your life that requires hope. Spend some time in prayer, asking for Mary's intercession to infuse this situation with the light of hope. Consider writing a prayer of hope, expressing your trust in God's plan and your desire to embrace this hope as Mary did. As a practical act of embodying hope, perform an act of kindness or encouragement for someone who may be struggling to find hope in their own life. Let this action be a testament to the power of hope shared.

Closing Prayer:

We thank You, Lord, for the gift of Mary, our Mother of Hope, who teaches us to trust in Your divine providence and to live with hope in all circumstances. Through her intercession, may we grow in our ability to see beyond the trials of the moment to the eternal joy promised to us through Christ. Keep us steadfast in hope, guided by Mary's example, as we journey towards the fulfillment of Your promises. Amen.

Day 22

Mary's Unwavering Faith

Opening Prayer:

O Holy Spirit, Fountain of Faith, and Blessed Virgin Mary, Exemplar of Trust, guide our hearts today on a journey towards deeper faith. Illuminate our path with the light of your wisdom, that we might learn from Mary's unwavering trust in God's promises.

Scripture Reading:

"In the sixth month the angel Gabriel was sent by God to a town in Galilee called Nazareth, to a virgin engaged to a man whose name was Joseph, of the house of David. The virgin's name was Mary. And he came to her and said, 'Greetings, favored one! The Lord is with you.' But she was much perplexed by his words and pondered what sort of greeting this might be. The angel said to her, 'Do not be afraid, Mary, for you have found favor with God. And now, you will conceive in your womb and bear a son, and you will name him Jesus. He will be great, and will be called the Son of the Most High, and the Lord God will give to him the throne of his ancestor David. He will reign over the house of Jacob forever, and of his kingdom there will be no end.' Mary said to the angel, 'How can this be, since I am a virgin?' The angel said to her, 'The Holy Spirit will come upon you, and the power of the Most High will overshadow you; therefore the child to be born will be holy; he will be called Son of God. And now, your relative Elizabeth in her old age has also conceived a son; and this is the sixth month for her who was said to be barren. For nothing will be impossible with God.' Then Mary said, 'Here am I, the servant of the Lord; let it be with me according to your word.' Then the angel departed from her."

Luke 1:26-38

Reflection:

At the Annunciation, Mary is presented with a message that would forever change the course of history—and her life. Her response, "Behold, I am the servant of the Lord; let it be to me according to your word," reflects a profound depth of faith and submission to God's will. This moment encapsulates the essence of true faith: trust in God even when the path ahead is unknown, and a willingness to say "yes" to His call, regardless of the cost. Mary's faith was not passive but an active, courageous commitment to participate in God's salvific plan. This invites us to reflect on our own faith journey. Are we willing to trust God with our lives, to say "yes" to Him without knowing where it might lead? How can Mary's example inspire us to live out our faith more fully, embracing God's will with open hearts?

Prayer of the Day:

Dear Mary, Mother of Faith, your response to the angel Gabriel shows us the beauty and strength of complete trust in God. Teach us to say "yes" to God with the same faith and courage that you did. Help us to trust in His promises, even when we do not understand His plans. Intercede for us, that our faith may be strengthened and our lives may reflect the trust and submission you showed. May we, like you, be bearers of Christ to the world through our faith and actions. Amen.

Spiritual Exercise:

Today, spend some time in prayer reflecting on an area of your life where you are being called to deeper faith and trust in God. Write down any fears or hesitations you have about surrendering this area fully to God. Offer these to Mary in prayer, asking for her intercession to help you say your own "fiat" to God's will. Consider taking one concrete step today as a sign of your willingness to trust God more fully, inspired by Mary's example.

Closing Prayer:

Lord God, we thank you for the gift of Mary, our model of faith, who teaches us to trust in You completely. Through her intercession, help us to grow in our faith and to live out our "yes" to You in every aspect of our lives. May our journey of faith draw us closer to You and to the fulfillment of Your will for us, just as it did for Mary. Keep us under the protective mantle of Mary, our mother, as we strive to live in humility and joy, trusting in Your love and mercy. Amen.

Day 23

Mary's Compassionate Heart

Opening Prayer:

O Holy Spirit, Wellspring of Compassion, and Blessed Virgin Mary, Mother of Compassion, guide our hearts today as we seek to embody the tenderness and love you show to all God's children. Help us to open our hearts to the needs of others, following your example of selfless care and compassion.

Scripture Reading:

"On the third day, there was a wedding in Cana of Galilee, and the mother of Jesus was there. Jesus and his disciples had also been invited to the wedding. When the wine gave out, the mother of Jesus said to him, 'They have no wine.' And Jesus said to her, 'Woman, what concern is that to you and to me? My hour has not yet come.' His mother said to the servants, 'Do whatever he tells you.'"

John 2:1-5

Reflection:

At the Wedding at Cana, Mary demonstrates her compassionate heart by noticing a need — the lack of wine — and taking action to address it, even before the hosts are aware of the impending embarrassment. Her intervention, "They have no wine," and her instruction to the servants, "Do whatever he tells you," showcase her attentiveness to others' needs and her trust in Jesus' power to meet those needs. This story highlights the beauty of Mary's compassionate heart, which is attuned to the sufferings and joys of those around her. It invites us to reflect on our own capacity for compassion. Are we attentive to the needs of those in our community? How can we, like Mary, act as mediators of God's grace and compassion in the world?

Prayer of the Day:

Dear Mary, Mother of Compassion, your awareness and action at the Wedding at Cana inspire us to be more attentive to the needs of those around us. Teach us to cultivate a heart of compassion, that we might see where love is needed and act to provide it. Help us to trust in Jesus as you did, knowing that through Him, our efforts to show love and compassion can bear abundant fruit. Intercede for us, that our lives may reflect the love and tenderness of your Son, Jesus Christ. Amen.

Spiritual Exercise:

Today, make a conscious effort to notice the needs of those around you, whether they are big or small. Choose one act of compassion you can perform — it could be offering a word of encouragement, helping someone with a task, or simply being present to someone who needs to talk. As you do this, keep Mary's example in mind, and offer your action as a prayer to God, asking for the grace to become more like Mary in your everyday life.

Closing Prayer:

We thank You, Lord, for the gift of Mary, our Mother of Compassion, who teaches us the value of being present to the needs of others. Through her example and intercession, help us to grow in love and compassion, reflecting Your love in all that we do. May our lives be a testament to the transformative power of Your love, guided by Mary's example. Keep us under her protective mantle, always drawing us closer to You through acts of kindness and compassion. Amen.

Day 24

Mary's Role in Divine Mercy

Opening Prayer:

O Holy Spirit, Fountain of Mercy, and Blessed Virgin Mary, Mother of Divine Mercy, guide us today as we reflect on the vastness of God's mercy and your role in manifesting this mercy to the world. Help us to open our hearts to receive and to become conduits of this inexhaustible mercy in our lives.

Scripture Reading:

"His mercy is for those who fear him

from generation to generation."

Luke 1:50

Reflection:

Mary's Magnificat is not only a song of praise but a profound declaration of God's mercy. Her words, "His mercy is for those who fear him from generation to generation," highlight the continuity and accessibility of God's mercy throughout all ages. Mary herself embodies this mercy, having been chosen to bring the Mercy Incarnate, Jesus Christ, into the world. This passage invites us to contemplate the role of Mary in the economy of salvation as the Mother of Mercy. How does understanding Mary's role enhance our appreciation for God's mercy? How can we, inspired by Mary, become more merciful towards ourselves and others, recognizing the boundless mercy God offers us?

Prayer of the Day:

Dear Mary, Mother of Mercy, your song of praise reminds us of the depth and breadth of God's mercy. Intercede for us, that we may always remember the mercy God extends to us, and be inspired to act mercifully towards others. Teach us to trust in God's mercy, to seek it for ourselves, and to embody it in our actions, just as you did by saying 'yes' to becoming the Mother of God. May our lives reflect the mercy and love of Jesus, whom you brought into the world. Amen.

Spiritual Exercise:

Today, take a moment to reflect on God's mercy in your own life. How have you experienced God's mercy? Write down a few instances and express your gratitude in prayer. Then, identify one way you can show mercy to someone else today — it could be through forgiveness, a kind act, or a word of encouragement. Let this action be a reflection of the mercy Mary spoke of in her Magnificat and a testament to the mercy of God that flows through generations.

Closing Prayer:

We thank You, Lord, for the gift of Your mercy, which is new every morning and sustains us through every trial. Through the intercession of the Blessed Virgin Mary, help us to be vessels of Your mercy, sharing it generously with all those we encounter. May our lives be a reflection of Your love and mercy, drawing others closer to You. Keep us under the protective mantle of Mary, our Mother of Mercy, as we strive to live in the light of Your love. Amen.

Day 25

Mary as the Model of Quiet Strength

Opening Prayer:

O Holy Spirit, Giver of Strength, and Blessed Virgin Mary, Emblem of Quiet Courage, lead us today on a path of inner strength and peace. May we learn from your example how to embody dignity and strength in our walk with God.

Scripture Reading:

"But Mary treasured all these words and pondered them in her heart."

Luke 2:19

Reflection:

In the quiet of her heart, Mary models a strength that is profound and contemplative. Unlike the worldly notion of strength, characterized by loud declarations and visible power, Mary's strength lies in her reflective and serene trust in God's plan. Her ability to treasure and ponder the events surrounding the birth of Jesus speaks to a deep, internal fortitude. This reflective posture allowed her to navigate the complexities of her role as the mother of the Messiah with grace and resilience. Mary's example invites us to consider the power of quiet strength in our own lives. How can we cultivate a similar inner fortitude that stands firm in faith and trust, despite the uncertainties and storms we face? How does Mary's quiet strength inspire us to reflect more deeply on the events of our lives, seeing them through the lens of God's providence?

Prayer of the Day:

Dear Mary, our serene and strong Mother, teach us the value of quiet strength and reflective trust in God's will. Help us to treasure the moments of our lives, both joyous and challenging, pondering them with faith and hope in our hearts. May your example of dignified strength inspire us to face our trials with a calm and steadfast heart, anchored in the trust that God is always with us, guiding and sustaining us through His love. Amen.

Spiritual Exercise:

Take some time today to reflect quietly on a current challenge or situation in your life. Sit in a peaceful place, free from distractions, and present this situation to Mary in prayer. Ask for her intercession to grant you the grace of quiet strength and trust in God's plan for you. Consider journaling your thoughts, feelings, and any insights that come to you during this time of reflection. As a practical application, identify one small action you can take this week to demonstrate quiet strength in the face of your challenges, inspired by Mary's example.

Closing Prayer:

We thank you, Lord, for the blessed example of Mary, who shows us the power of quiet strength and deep trust in your will. Through her intercession, grant us the grace to face our lives with the same serene courage and reflective faith. May our hearts always be open to your guidance, and may we walk in the footsteps of Mary, our Mother, with dignity and strength. Keep us under her protective mantle, that we might grow closer to you in all that we do. Amen.

Day 26

Mary, Model of Perseverance

Opening Prayer:

O Holy Spirit, Guide on our journey, and Blessed Virgin Mary, Exemplar of Perseverance, inspire us today as we reflect on the virtue of steadfastness in faith and life. Strengthen our resolve to follow God's will with unwavering commitment, as you did.

Scripture Reading:

"Now every year his parents went to Jerusalem for the festival of the Passover. And when he was twelve years old, they went up as usual for the festival. When the festival was ended and they started to return, the boy Jesus stayed behind in Jerusalem, but his parents did not know it. Assuming that he was in the group of travelers, they went a day's journey. Then they started to look for him among their relatives and friends. When they did not find him, they returned to Jerusalem to search for him. After three days they found him in the temple, sitting among the teachers, listening to them and asking them questions. And all who heard him were amazed at his understanding and his answers. When his parents saw him they were astonished; and his mother said to him, 'Child, why have you treated us like this? Look, your father and I have been searching for you in great anxiety.' He said to them, 'Why were you searching for me? Did you not know that I must be in my Father's house?' But they did not understand what he said to them. Then he went down with them and came to Nazareth, and was obedient to them. His mother treasured all these things in her heart. And Jesus increased in wisdom and in years, and in divine and human favor."

A Pilgrimage in Prayer

Luke 2:41-52

Reflection:

In this passage, Mary and Joseph's search for Jesus, who stayed behind in the Temple, showcases Mary's perseverance in faith and motherhood. Her distress upon realizing Jesus was not with them, and her subsequent relief and gentle reprimand when finding Him, highlight her human experience of worry and relief. This episode illustrates Mary's steadfast faith and her perseverance through the challenges of raising Jesus. Mary's response to Jesus' explanation, though not fully understanding, "But his mother treasured all these things in her heart," signifies her deep, reflective faith and her commitment to pondering the mysteries of His life. This invites us to consider our own journey of faith. How do we respond to the incomprehensible or unexpected turns in our life? Are we willing to persevere in faith, even when we do not understand God's plan?

Prayer of the Day:

Dear Mary, our Mother of Perseverance, your journey through the joys and trials of motherhood and discipleship is a beacon of hope for us. Teach us to persevere in our faith, especially in moments of doubt and confusion. Help us to treasure God's presence in our lives, reflecting on His actions and words with a heart open to understanding. May we, like you, remain steadfast in our journey towards God, trusting in His plan for us. Amen.

Spiritual Exercise:

Identify an area in your life where you are struggling to persevere — it could be a personal goal, a spiritual practice, or a relationship that requires patience and commitment. Offer this intention to Mary in prayer, asking for her guidance and strength to persevere. As a practical step, commit to one action today that symbolizes your dedication to perseverance, whether it's renewing your effort in prayer, reaching out to reconcile with someone, or taking a small step towards a goal you've set. Reflect on Mary's example of perseverance and allow it to inspire your actions.

Closing Prayer:

Lord God, we thank You for the gift of Mary, who teaches us the value of perseverance in faith and life. Through her example and intercession, grant us the grace to face our challenges with courage and trust in Your divine will. May we walk in her footsteps, keeping our hearts and minds fixed on You, as we journey through the complexities of life. Keep us under the protective mantle of Mary, our Mother, as we strive to live in fidelity to You. Amen.

Day 27

Mary, Our Guide in Prayer

Opening Prayer:

O Holy Spirit, Source of Prayer, and Blessed Virgin Mary, Guide in our journey towards God, direct our hearts and minds today as we seek to deepen our relationship with the Lord through prayer. May your example inspire us to a life of constant conversation with God.

Scripture Reading:

"After three days they found him in the temple, sitting among the teachers, listening to them and asking them questions. And all who heard him were amazed at his understanding and his answers. When his parents[a] saw him they were astonished; and his mother said to him, 'Child, why have you treated us like this? Look, your father and I have been searching for you in great anxiety.' He said to them, 'Why were you searching for me? Did you not know that I must be in my Father's house?' But they did not understand what he said to them. Then he went down with them and came to Nazareth, and was obedient to them. His mother treasured all these things in her heart."

Luke 2:46-51

Reflection:

This passage reveals Mary's deep commitment to her son and her faith. Finding Jesus in the Temple after three days of anxious searching, Mary and Joseph are astonished to find Him discussing with the teachers. Jesus' response to Mary, "Did you not know that I must be in my Father's house?" highlights not only His divine mission but also Mary's role in guiding us towards understanding the importance of being in the presence of God. Mary's contemplation of these events in her heart teaches us the value of meditative prayer and reflection on the mysteries of Christ's life. How does Mary's example encourage us to seek Jesus diligently in our lives? How can we, like Mary, treasure and ponder the presence and words of Jesus in our hearts?

Prayer of the Day:

Dear Mary, our Guide in Prayer, teach us to seek Jesus with all our hearts, finding Him in the quiet of our prayers and the depths of our daily lives. Help us to understand the importance of being in the presence of God, as you did throughout your life. May we learn to treasure and ponder the mysteries of Christ's love and mission, growing in intimacy with Him through prayer. Intercede for us, that our prayer life may become a true reflection of our desire to be close to God. Amen.

Spiritual Exercise:

Dedicate a special time today for silent prayer or meditation, focusing on the presence of Jesus in your life. Reflect on a particular event in the Gospels that speaks to you deeply, and like Mary, ponder its meaning in your heart. Consider keeping a prayer journal to note any insights, feelings, or resolutions that arise during this time of prayer. As a practical application, try to incorporate a short period of meditative prayer into your daily routine, using Mary's example as a guide to deepen your relationship with Jesus.

Closing Prayer:

We thank You, Lord, for the blessed Virgin Mary, who teaches us the depth and beauty of a life devoted to prayer. Through her intercession, may we grow in our love for You, seeking Your presence with all our hearts and pondering Your words and actions in our lives. Help us to follow Mary's example, leading us closer to You through prayerful reflection and devotion. Keep us under the protective mantle of Mary, our mother and guide, as we strive to live each day in closer communion with You. Amen.

Day 28

Mary's Intercession in Our Lives

Opening Prayer:

O Holy Spirit, Giver of Grace, and Blessed Virgin Mary, our Advocate and Intercessor, guide our hearts and minds today as we reflect on the power of your intercession and the comfort it brings to our spiritual journey. Lead us closer to your Son, Jesus, through your maternal care.

Scripture Reading:

"On the third day there was a wedding in Cana of Galilee, and the mother of Jesus was there. Jesus and his disciples had also been invited to the wedding. When the wine gave out, the mother of Jesus said to him, 'They have no wine.' And Jesus said to her, 'Woman, what concern is that to you and to me? My hour has not yet come.' His mother said to the servants, 'Do whatever he tells you.' Now standing there were six stone water jars for the Jewish rites of purification, each holding twenty or thirty gallons. Jesus said to them, 'Fill the jars with water.' And they filled them up to the brim. He said to them, 'Now draw some out, and take it to the chief steward.' So they took it. When the steward tasted the water that had become wine, and did not know where it came from (though the servants who had drawn the water knew), the steward called the bridegroom and said to him, 'Everyone serves the good wine first, and then the inferior wine after the guests have become drunk. But you have kept the good wine until now.' Jesus did this, the first of his signs, in Cana of Galilee, and revealed his glory; and his disciples believed in him."

John 2:1-11

Reflection:

The Wedding at Cana presents a profound instance of Mary's intercession, where her observance and action lead to Jesus performing His first miracle. Mary's simple request, "They have no wine," and her direction to the servants, "Do whatever he tells you," underscore her role as mediator between our needs and Christ's merciful response. This event not only highlights Mary's compassion and understanding of human needs but also her trust in Jesus' power and willingness to help us. It invites us to reflect on the significance of Mary's intercession in our own lives. How do we approach Mary in prayer, and how can we be more open to her guidance towards Jesus? In what ways can we trust more deeply in the efficacy of her intercession for our needs and those of the whole world?

Prayer of the Day:

Dear Blessed Virgin Mary, through your powerful intercession at Cana, you showed us the way to bring our needs before Jesus, trusting in His kindness and mercy. Help us to come to you with confidence, knowing that you are our mother and advocate, always ready to listen and to guide us to your Son. Teach us to say, "Do whatever he tells you," with the same faith and obedience that you demonstrated. Intercede for us in all our needs, especially those we hold deep within our hearts. Amen.

Spiritual Exercise:

Reflect on a particular need or intention in your life where you seek Mary's intercession. Dedicate some time today to pray the Rosary, focusing on the mysteries that resonate with your current situation, offering each Hail Mary as a petition for her guidance and intercession. Alternatively, write a prayer or letter to Mary, expressing your needs and asking for her maternal intercession. Trust that, just as at the Wedding at Cana, Mary presents our needs to Jesus, who responds with generosity and love.

Closing Prayer:

We thank You, Lord, for giving us Mary as our mother and intercessor, who leads us to You with her example and prayers. Through her intercession, may we experience Your grace and mercy in abundance, and may our faith be strengthened. Help us to always seek Mary's guidance on our journey towards You, confident in her love and support. May her intercession bring us closer to You, transforming our lives with Your divine love. Keep us under the protective mantle of Mary, guiding us ever closer to Your heart. Amen.

Day 29

Embracing Mary's Humility

Opening Prayer:

O Holy Spirit, Teacher of Truth, and Blessed Virgin Mary, Model of Humility, guide us today as we seek to embrace the virtue of humility in our lives. May we learn from your example, Mary, to live with a heart open to God's grace and guidance.

Scripture Reading:

"For he has looked with favor on the lowliness of his servant.

Surely, from now on all generations will call me blessed."

Luke 1:48

Reflection:

Mary's response to the Annunciation, as captured in her Magnificat, shines a light on the beauty and strength of humility. Recognizing herself as "the humble estate of his servant," Mary accepts God's plan with both humility and joy. Her humility does not stem from a sense of unworthiness but from an understanding of her role in God's grand design. This moment invites us to reflect on our approach to humility. Do we see humility as weakness or as the true strength it is? How can we, like Mary, live in humility, acknowledging God's greatness and our dependence on His mercy and love?

Prayer of the Day:

Dear Mary, our humble Mother, teach us the true meaning of humility — not as self-degradation but as a joyful acceptance of our role in God's plan. Help us to live with the grace and humility you showed, recognizing our own limitations while trusting fully in God's power and goodness. May your example inspire us to serve God and others with a humble heart, ever mindful of the blessings that humility brings into our lives. Amen.

Spiritual Exercise:

Today, choose an area of your life where you can practice humility — perhaps in acknowledging someone else's contribution, asking for help when needed, or stepping back to let others shine. Reflect on this act of humility and consider journaling about the experience. How did it make you feel? What did you learn from it? Let this act be a small step towards embracing humility more fully in your daily life, inspired by Mary's example.

Closing Prayer:

We thank You, Lord, for the gift of Mary, who teaches us the power and beauty of humility. Through her intercession, grant us the grace to grow in humility, recognizing Your greatness and our need for Your guidance. May our lives reflect the humble service and love that Mary lived every day, drawing us closer to You and to the life You call us to live. Keep us under the protective mantle of Mary, our guide and mother, as we strive to live in humility and joy. Amen.

Day 30

Mary's Faithful Obedience

Opening Prayer:

O Holy Spirit, Guide of our paths, and Blessed Virgin Mary, Exemplar of Obedience, enlighten our journey today as we seek to understand and emulate the depth of your obedience to God's will. May we learn from you, Mary, how to listen and respond to God with a heart full of trust and submission.

Scripture Reading:

"Then Mary said, 'Here am I, the servant of the Lord; let it be with me according to your word.' Then the angel departed from her."

Luke 1:38

Reflection:

Mary's response to the Annunciation encapsulates the essence of faithful obedience. Faced with a divine mission that would undoubtedly transform her life, Mary embraces God's will with humility and courage. Her simple yet profound "yes" to God is a testament to her deep faith and trust in the Lord's plan for her life and for the salvation of the world. This moment challenges us to reflect on our own response to God's call. Are we willing to submit to God's will with the same faith and obedience as Mary? How can her example inspire us to approach our life's decisions, big or small, with an attitude of openness and trust in God's guidance?

Prayer of the Day:

Dear Mary, Mother of Yes, your unwavering obedience to God's will is a beacon of light for us in our journey of faith. Teach us to say "yes" to God with the same trust and openness that you showed at the Annunciation. Help us to discern God's will in our lives and to respond with joyful obedience, trusting that He leads us towards our ultimate good. May your example of faithful submission inspire us to live our lives in service to God and to one another. Amen.

Spiritual Exercise:

Take a moment today to reflect on an area of your life where you might be resisting God's will or struggling to trust in His plan. Pray for the grace of obedience and trust, asking Mary to guide you in saying your own "yes" to God. Consider writing a prayer of commitment to God, expressing your desire to follow Him more closely and to trust in His will for your life. As a practical application, choose one small way to act on this commitment today, whether it's through a specific act of service, making a difficult decision you've been postponing, or simply spending additional time in prayer.

Closing Prayer:

Lord God, we thank You for the gift of Mary, whose faithful obedience brought Your Son into the world for our salvation. Through her example and intercession, strengthen our resolve to follow Your will with trust and joy. Grant us the courage to say "yes" to You, no matter the cost, trusting that Your ways lead us to true freedom and joy. Keep us under the loving mantle of Mary, our mother, as we strive to live each day in faithful obedience to You. Amen.

A Pilgrimage in Prayer

Day 31

Mary's Journey of Faith

Opening Prayer:

O Holy Spirit, Guide on our spiritual journey, and Blessed Virgin Mary, Beacon of Faith, illuminate our path today as we seek to follow your example of unwavering faith and trust in God's plan. May we learn from your journey, embracing each step with faith and love.

Scripture Reading:

"Now after they had left, an angel of the Lord appeared to Joseph in a dream and said, 'Get up, take the child and his mother, and flee to Egypt, and remain there until I tell you; for Herod is about to search for the child, to destroy him.' Then Joseph[a] got up, took the child and his mother by night, and went to Egypt, and remained there until the death of Herod. This was to fulfill what had been spoken by the Lord through the prophet, 'Out of Egypt I have called my son.'"

Matthew 2:13-15

Reflection:

Mary's life was marked by moments of profound faith, perhaps none so dramatic as the flight into Egypt. Faced with the threat to her child's life, Mary, along with Joseph, embarked on a difficult journey, trusting in God's protection and guidance. This episode is a testament to Mary's strength, courage, and deep faith in God's promises. It invites us to reflect on our own journey of faith. How do we respond when faced with challenges or when God's plan seems uncertain? Are we willing to step out in faith, trusting in God's guidance and protection, as Mary did?

Prayer of the Day:

Dear Mary, our Mother of Faith, your journey to Egypt with your Holy Family is a powerful example of trust in God's providence. Teach us to embrace our own spiritual journey with the same faith and courage you showed. Help us to trust in God's guidance, especially in moments of uncertainty and fear. May we, like you, be guided by the light of faith, always moving forward in the assurance of God's love and protection. Amen.

Spiritual Exercise:

Reflect on a time in your life when you had to make a difficult decision or take a step into the unknown, trusting in God's guidance. How did your faith influence your decision? Spend some time in prayer, asking for Mary's intercession to strengthen your faith for future challenges. As a practical application, consider writing a letter to Mary, sharing your current fears or challenges and asking for her guidance and protection. Let this act of writing be a prayerful offering, entrusting your journey to her maternal care.

Closing Prayer:

Lord God, we thank You for the gift of Mary, who walked a path of faith and trust in Your divine will. Through her intercession, grant us the grace to face our own journey with courage and faith, trusting in Your guidance and protection. May we draw inspiration from Mary's example, living our lives in faithful service to You and to others. Keep us under the loving care of Mary, our mother, as we continue our pilgrimage towards Your eternal kingdom. Amen.

Day 32

Mary's Loving Presence in Times of Need

Opening Prayer:

O Holy Spirit, Source of Comfort, and Blessed Virgin Mary, Mother of Consolation, guide our hearts and minds today as we seek solace in your loving presence. Illuminate our path with the light of your compassion, helping us to feel your maternal care in every moment of our lives.

Scripture Reading:

"And that is what the soldiers did. Meanwhile, standing near the cross of Jesus were his mother, and his mother's sister, Mary the wife of Clopas, and Mary Magdalene. When Jesus saw his mother and the disciple whom he loved standing beside her, he said to his mother, 'Woman, here is your son.' Then he said to the disciple, 'Here is your mother.' And from that hour the disciple took her into his own home."

John 19:25-27

Reflection:

Standing by the cross, Mary embodies the pinnacle of maternal love and spiritual presence in the midst of unimaginable pain and sorrow. Her steadfast presence at the foot of the cross speaks volumes about her unwavering support and love for Jesus, even in the face of great personal loss. This poignant moment invites us to reflect on the nature of Mary's loving presence in our own lives, especially during times of trial and need. How does Mary's example inspire us to seek her intercession and comfort in our moments of despair? How can we emulate her strength and love in supporting others around us who are suffering?

Prayer of the Day:

Dear Mary, our Mother of Sorrows, your courage and love at the foot of the cross are a beacon of hope and comfort for us all. In our times of need, remind us that we are never alone, and that your maternal care extends to each of us, offering solace and strength. Teach us to turn to you with trust, knowing that through your intercession, Jesus provides the grace we need to endure and overcome our trials. May we, inspired by your example, be a source of comfort and support to those around us who are suffering. Amen.

Spiritual Exercise:

Today, reflect on a situation in your life where you need Mary's loving presence and intercession. Take some time to pray the Hail Mary, focusing on each word, and imagining Mary standing with you in your current trials, offering her love and support. Consider reaching out to someone in your life who may be experiencing their own time of need, offering them a listening ear, a word of encouragement, or a simple act of kindness. Let this action be a reflection of Mary's love and compassion, channeled through you.

Closing Prayer:

We thank You, Lord, for giving us Mary, a model of love and support, especially in times of great need. Through her example and intercession, help us to remember that we are never alone in our suffering. Grant us the grace to find comfort in Mary's embrace and to extend that same love and support to others in need. May we always feel the protective mantle of Mary around us, guiding us closer to You, our source of eternal consolation. Amen.

Day 33

Mary as a Beacon of Hope

Opening Prayer:

O Holy Spirit, Bringer of Hope, and Blessed Virgin Mary, Beacon of Hope to all who seek your intercession, guide our hearts today towards the light of Christ that you reflect so perfectly. May we draw inspiration from your unwavering faith and be filled with hope in God's promises.

Scripture Reading:

"On the third day, there was a wedding in Cana of Galilee, and the mother of Jesus was there. Jesus and his disciples had also been invited to the wedding. When the wine gave out, the mother of Jesus said to him, 'They have no wine.' And Jesus said to her, 'Woman, what concern is that to you and to me? My hour has not yet come.' His mother said to the servants, 'Do whatever he tells you.' Now standing there were six stone water jars for the Jewish rites of purification, each holding twenty or thirty gallons. Jesus said to them, 'Fill the jars with water.' And they filled them up to the brim. He said to them, 'Now draw some out, and take it to the chief steward.' So they took it. When the steward tasted the water that had become wine and did not know where it came from (though the servants who had drawn the water knew), the steward called the bridegroom and said to him, 'Everyone serves the good wine first, and then the inferior wine after the guests have become drunk. But you have kept the good wine until now.' Jesus did this, the first of his signs, in Cana of Galilee, and revealed his glory; and his disciples believed in him."

John 2:1-11

Reflection:

The Wedding at Cana not only showcases Mary's role in Jesus' first miracle but also her function as a beacon of hope for those in need. Her observation, "They have no wine," followed by her confidence in Jesus to resolve the situation, highlights her deep faith and her ability to inspire hope in others. This miracle, prompted by Mary's intercession, serves as a powerful reminder of the transformative power of hope and faith in God's providence. Mary's actions invite us to consider how we can be beacons of hope in our own communities. How does Mary inspire us to act with faith and hope in challenging situations? How can we, like Mary, encourage others to trust in Jesus' power to change circumstances and hearts?

Prayer of the Day:

Dear Mary, our Hope, through your faith and intercession at Cana, you showed us the power of trusting in Jesus. Help us to embody the hope you have in God's promises, especially in moments of uncertainty and need. Teach us to turn to Jesus with confidence, as you did, and to be instruments of hope for those around us. May your example guide us to live with a hopeful heart, trusting in the Lord's timing and mercy. Amen.

Spiritual Exercise:

Today, reflect on a situation in your life or in the life of someone you know that requires hope. Pray for Mary's intercession, asking for the faith to trust in God's providence and for the grace to be a beacon of hope to others. Consider performing an act of kindness or offering a word of encouragement to someone who may be in need of hope. Let this action be a testament to the hope that Mary exemplifies, and a reflection of your trust in God's loving care.

A Pilgrimage in Prayer

Closing Prayer:

We thank You, Lord, for the gift of Mary, our Mother of Hope, who leads us to Your Son, the source of all hope. Through her example and prayers, fill us with a hopeful spirit, that we may trust in Your promises and extend Your love and hope to all we encounter. Keep us under the protective mantle of Mary, that we might always be guided by her light and live in the hope of Your salvation. Amen.

Day 34

Mary's Compassionate Heart

Opening Prayer:

O Holy Spirit, Fountain of Love, and Blessed Virgin Mary, Mother of Compassion, guide our hearts today as we seek to embody the compassion and love you showed throughout your life. May we be inspired by your example to live with hearts open to the needs of others.

Scripture Reading:

"When Jesus saw his mother and the disciple whom he loved standing beside her, he said to his mother, 'Woman, here is your son.' Then he said to the disciple, 'Here is your mother.' And from that hour, the disciple took her into his own home."

John 19:26-27

Reflection:

At the foot of the cross, amidst her own profound sorrow, Mary's heart remained open to love and compassion, accepting John as her son. This act of compassion at a moment of great personal loss highlights Mary's immense capacity for love and her role as a mother to all believers. Her willingness to embrace others in their own time of need, even as she faced the ultimate loss, offers a powerful lesson on the depth of compassionate love. How does Mary's example challenge us to open our hearts to those around us, especially in moments of suffering? How can we follow her model of compassion in our daily lives, extending our love to those in need of care and understanding?

Prayer of the Day:

Dear Mary, Mother of Compassion, your heart, so full of love and tenderness, teaches us the true meaning of compassion. Pray for us, that we may learn to live with the same open-hearted generosity, reaching out to embrace those who suffer, offering them the comfort and care they need. May your example inspire us to acts of kindness and compassion, that we might reflect the love of your Son, Jesus, in our interactions with others. Amen.

Spiritual Exercise:

Identify someone in your life or community who is experiencing hardship, loneliness, or suffering. Consider a concrete way you can offer them compassion and support today, whether through a kind word, a helpful deed, or simply your presence and listening ear. Let this act of compassion be a reflection of Mary's loving heart, and a step towards living out the call to love and care for one another as she did.

Closing Prayer:

We thank You, Lord, for the gift of Mary, whose compassionate heart serves as a model for our own. Through her example and intercession, help us to grow in love and compassion, that we might be a source of comfort and hope to those around us. May our lives echo her love, drawing others closer to You, the source of all comfort and peace. Keep us under the protective mantle of Mary, our mother, as we strive to live in service to You and to one another. Amen.

Day 35

Mary's Role as a Disciple

Opening Prayer:

O Holy Spirit, Enlightener of Hearts, and Blessed Virgin Mary, Model Disciple, guide our hearts and minds as we embark upon today's journey of reflection. May we learn from your example, Mary, to live as true disciples of Christ, following Him with courage and love.

Scripture Reading:

"But Mary treasured all these words and pondered them in her heart."

Luke 2:19

Reflection:

Mary's contemplative response to the events surrounding the birth of Jesus highlights her role as the first and model disciple. Her deep reflection on these mysteries shows us the importance of meditating on God's Word and actions in our lives. Mary's ability to treasure and ponder the works of God is a lesson in discipleship, teaching us to be attentive to the divine presence and to carry Jesus in our hearts. How can we, like Mary, become more reflective and contemplative in our faith journey? How does Mary's example inspire us to treasure and ponder God's presence and action in our lives, and how can this deepen our discipleship?

1 Prayer of the Day:

Dear Mary, Teach of Discipleship, you who carried Jesus in your womb and in your heart, teach us to treasure the gift of faith as you did. Help us to ponder the mysteries of Christ's life, death, and resurrection, drawing ever closer to Him through prayer and meditation. Guide us in our journey of faith, that we may follow your example and grow in our understanding and love of the Lord. May we, like you, be true disciples, bearing Christ to the world with joy and faithfulness. Amen.

Spiritual Exercise:

Take some time today for quiet reflection or meditation on a passage from the Gospels that speaks to you. Consider how Mary might have lived out the message of this passage in her own life as a disciple. Journal your thoughts, feelings, and any resolutions that arise from this time of reflection. As a practical application, choose one aspect of Mary's discipleship that you would like to emulate in your own life — perhaps her contemplative spirit, her unconditional yes to God, or her courage — and take one small step today to live out that aspect.

Closing Prayer:

We thank You, Lord, for the blessed Virgin Mary, who shows us the way to be true disciples of Christ. Through her example and intercession, help us to grow in love and devotion to You. May our lives reflect her discipleship, that we may bring the light of Christ to all we meet. Keep us under the protective mantle of Mary, our mother and guide, as we strive to live out our call to follow Jesus. Amen.

Day 36

Mary's Gaze of Love and Sorrow

Opening Prayer:

O Holy Spirit, Comforter of the Afflicted, and Blessed Virgin Mary, whose gaze of love and sorrow pierced the mystery of suffering, guide our hearts and minds as we reflect upon the depth of your compassion and courage. Teach us to look upon the world and our own sufferings with the same love and faith.

Scripture Reading:

"And that is what the soldiers did. Meanwhile, standing near the cross of Jesus were his mother, and his mother's sister, Mary the wife of Clopas, and Mary Magdalene. When Jesus saw his mother and the disciple whom he loved standing beside her, he said to his mother, 'Woman, here is your son.' Then he said to the disciple, 'Here is your mother.' And from that hour the disciple took her into his own home."

John 19:25-27

Reflection:

As we contemplate Mary standing near the cross, her gaze upon her crucified son embodies a profound mixture of love, sorrow, and unwavering faith. This moment invites us to meditate on the significance of Mary's gaze — a gaze that fully embraces the pain and suffering of her Son for the salvation of the world. Mary's presence at the foot of the cross teaches us about the strength found in vulnerability and the power of love to endure the greatest of sorrows. How does Mary's example of steadfast faith and love in the face of suffering inspire us in our own trials? How can we cultivate a gaze that reflects Mary's compassion and hope when faced with the crosses in our own lives or in the lives of those around us?

Prayer of the Day:

Dear Mary, Our Lady of Sorrows, your gaze at the foot of the cross is a testament to the depth of your love and the strength of your faith. Help us to learn from your example, that we may face our own sorrows with courage and love. Intercede for us, that we may have the grace to stand by those who suffer, offering them the consolation and hope found in Christ. May your maternal gaze inspire us to see the world with eyes full of compassion and faith. Amen.

Spiritual Exercise:

Spend some time in quiet reflection or before a crucifix, contemplating the scene at Calvary. Imagine Mary's gaze upon Jesus and reflect on what her thoughts and prayers might have been. Consider writing a prayer or letter to Mary, expressing your desires to cultivate a gaze of love and faith in the midst of your own trials or in solidarity with those who suffer. As a practical action, reach out to someone who is experiencing their own crucifixion moment, offering them your presence, support, and love, as Mary did for Jesus.

Closing Prayer:

Gracious God, we thank You for the gift of Mary, whose gaze at the cross teaches us about love, sorrow, and the redemptive power of suffering. Through her intercession, grant us the strength to embrace our crosses with faith and to offer our sufferings in union with Christ for the salvation of the world. May we, inspired by Mary's example, become beacons of hope and love in a world marked by pain and loss.

Keep us under the protective gaze of Mary, our mother, as we strive to live and love like Jesus. Amen.

A Pilgrimage in Prayer

Day 37

At the Foot of the Cross

Opening Prayer:

O Holy Spirit, Source of Strength, and Blessed Virgin Mary, steadfast at the foot of the Cross, guide our hearts and minds as we reflect upon the profound mystery of your sorrow and faith. Grant us the grace to stand firm in our trials, drawing strength from your example of unwavering love and trust in God's will.

Scripture Reading:

"And that is what the soldiers did. Meanwhile, standing near the cross of Jesus were his mother, and his mother's sister, Mary the wife of Clopas, and Mary Magdalene. When Jesus saw his mother and the disciple whom he loved standing beside her, he said to his mother, 'Woman, here is your son.' Then he said to the disciple, 'Here is your mother.' And from that hour the disciple took her into his own home."

John 19:25-27

Reflection:

Mary's presence at the foot of the Cross represents a pinnacle of faith and maternal love, witnessing the suffering and death of her Son for the salvation of humanity. This scene invites us to meditate on the depth of Mary's sorrow, coupled with her deep faith in God's promise. Mary's strength to stand at the foot of the Cross teaches us about the courage that comes from faith, the power of presence in moments of profound suffering, and the unconditional love that endures even the darkest trials. How does Mary's steadfast presence at the Cross inspire us to face our own crosses? How can we, like Mary, remain faithful and present to those enduring suffering, offering our love, support, and prayers as she did?

Prayer of the Day:

Dear Mary, Mother at the Foot of the Cross, your courage and faith in the face of unimaginable sorrow inspire us to carry our crosses with grace. Help us to stand by those who suffer, offering them the solace of our presence and the comfort of our prayers, just as you stood by Jesus. May we, inspired by your example, embody the love and strength found in the shadow of the Cross, trusting in the resurrection promise. Amen.

Spiritual Exercise:

Reflect on a time when you have experienced or witnessed suffering. How can you offer your presence and support as Mary did at the Cross? Consider reaching out to someone going through a difficult time, offering a listening ear, a comforting word, or a prayerful presence. Let this act of compassion be a living testament to the strength and love that Mary shows us.

Closing Prayer:

Lord Jesus, we thank you for the gift of your mother, Mary, who stood by the Cross as a witness to your love and sacrifice for us. Through her intercession, strengthen us in our moments of trial and suffering. May her example inspire us to live with courage and love, standing in solidarity with those who suffer, and always trusting in your redeeming love. Amen.

Day 38

Mary's Faith Beyond the Cross

Opening Prayer:

O Holy Spirit, Giver of Life, and Blessed Virgin Mary, Mother of Hope, guide our hearts and minds as we journey with you beyond the sorrow of the Cross to the dawn of the Resurrection. May our faith be strengthened by your example of unwavering trust in God's promise.

Scripture Reading:

"Early on the first day of the week, while it was still dark, Mary Magdalene came to the tomb and saw that the stone had been removed from the tomb. So she ran and went to Simon Peter and the other disciple, the one whom Jesus loved, and said to them, 'They have taken the Lord out of the tomb, and we do not know where they have laid him.'"

John 20:1-2

Reflection:

Though not directly mentioned at the tomb on Easter morning, Mary, the Mother of Jesus, embodies the faith and hope that all believers are called to hold onto in the darkness before dawn. Her journey did not end at the Cross; it extended into the profound mystery of the Resurrection. Reflecting on Mary's journey invites us to consider our own moments of waiting in darkness for the light of Christ to break forth. How does Mary's faith through the darkest of times inspire us to hold fast to hope, even when the dawn seems far away? How can we live out this Resurrection faith in our daily lives, especially in moments of doubt or despair?

Prayer of the Day:

Dear Mary, Mother of the Risen Lord, your faith and hope in the face of despair and darkness inspire us to look beyond our crosses to the promise of the Resurrection. Teach us to hold onto hope, to trust in God's unfailing love and power to bring life from death. May your example guide us to live as people of the Resurrection, radiating the joy and hope of your Son's victory over sin and death in our world today. Amen.

Spiritual Exercise:

Reflect on an area of your life where you are experiencing "darkness" or waiting for a "resurrection." Pray for Mary's intercession, that you may be granted the faith and hope to trust in God's timing and plan for this situation. Consider performing an act of kindness or offering a prayer for someone else who is in a period of waiting or suffering, as a sign of solidarity and hope in the Resurrection.

Closing Prayer:

Lord Jesus, we thank You for the gift of Your mother, Mary, who stood by the Cross and awaited the Resurrection with steadfast faith. Through her intercession, fill us with the same hope and trust in Your promise of new life. May we, inspired by her example, be bearers of Your light and love in a world that yearns for the hope of the Resurrection. Keep us under the loving protection of Mary, our mother, as we journey through our own trials towards the joy of Your eternal life. Amen.

Day 39

Mary as the New Eve

Opening Prayer:

O Holy Spirit, Bringer of Wisdom, and Blessed Virgin Mary, New Eve, guide our hearts and minds today as we seek to understand the depth of your role in God's plan of salvation. Illuminate our path with the light of your example, teaching us obedience, faith, and surrender to God's will.

Scripture Reading:

"When Jesus saw his mother and the disciple whom he loved standing beside her, he said to his mother, 'Woman, here is your son.' Then he said to the disciple, 'Here is your mother.' And from that hour the disciple took her into his own home."

John 19:26-27

Reflection:

Mary stands at the crossroads of salvation history as the New Eve, a title that signifies her pivotal role in God's redeeming work. Just as Eve's disobedience led to the fall, Mary's fiat marked the beginning of restoration and grace. Through her yes to God, Mary became the mother of all living in the new creation inaugurated by Christ. Her presence at the foot of the cross and her acceptance of John as her son symbolize the birth of the Church, the family of believers. In this way, Mary's spiritual motherhood extends to all who follow Christ. How does the parallel between Eve and Mary deepen our understanding of

Mary's role in our lives? How can we, as members of the Church, embrace Mary as our spiritual mother?

Prayer of the Day:

Dear Mary, New Eve and Mother of the Church, your unwavering faith and obedience brought light into a world darkened by sin. Pray for us, that we may follow your example of humble submission to God's will. Help us to embrace you as our spiritual mother, guiding us closer to your Son and nurturing our faith with your tender care. May your intercession lead us to live as true children of God, heirs of the promise of salvation. Amen.

Spiritual Exercise:

Reflect on Mary's role as your spiritual mother. Consider how you might cultivate a closer relationship with her, perhaps through prayer, meditation on the mysteries of the Rosary, or reading about her life and virtues. As a practical action, commit to a specific devotion or prayer to Mary this week, asking for her guidance and protection as you seek to live out your faith more fully.

Closing Prayer:

We thank you, Heavenly Father, for the gift of Mary, the New Eve, whose obedience and faith opened the way for our redemption. Through her intercession, strengthen us in faith and guide us on our journey towards you. May our lives bear witness to the love and grace that flow from her maternal heart, leading us ever closer to her Son, our Lord Jesus Christ. Amen.

Day 40

The Culmination of the Journey

Opening Prayer:

O Holy Spirit, Wellspring of Life, and Blessed Virgin Mary, Queen of Heaven and Earth, as we conclude this pilgrimage in prayer, we thank you for the grace that has accompanied us on this journey. Enlighten our hearts and minds, that we may carry the fruits of this spiritual odyssey into our daily lives, drawing ever closer to you and your Son.

Scripture Reading:

"A great portent appeared in heaven: a woman clothed with the sun, with the moon under her feet, and on her head a crown of twelve stars."

Revelation 12:1

Reflection:

As we reach the end of our forty-day pilgrimage with the Virgin Mary, we turn our gaze to the image of Mary as the Woman of the Apocalypse, crowned with stars and robed with the sun. This image symbolizes Mary's exalted role in salvation history and her ongoing intercession for the Church. It reminds us of the victory Christ has won over sin and death, and Mary's participation in this triumph. Reflecting on this journey, how has your relationship with Mary deepened? How does the image of Mary as Queen of Heaven inspire you to live out your calling as a disciple of Christ? How can you continue to seek Mary's intercession and guidance in your faith journey beyond these forty days?

Prayer of the Day:

Heavenly Queen, clothed in light and crowned with stars, we stand in awe of the mystery of your role in God's plan of salvation. As we conclude this pilgrimage, we entrust ourselves to your maternal care. Guide us in the way of humility, service, and profound faith. May our lives be a testament to the love and grace we have encountered on this journey with you. Intercede for us, that we may faithfully follow your Son and contribute to the building of His Kingdom.

Spiritual Exercise:

Choose a specific devotion to Mary that you will continue to practice beyond these forty days, such as daily Rosary, the Angelus, or the Memorare. Commit to an act of service or kindness in Mary's honor, reflecting her love and compassion. Consider journaling about your experience of this pilgrimage, noting any insights or changes in your spiritual life that have occurred.

Closing Prayer:

We thank you, Almighty God, for the gift of this spiritual pilgrimage with the Blessed Virgin Mary. May the lessons learned and the grace received during these forty days bear fruit in our lives. Help us to remain faithful to the teachings of your Church and to the example of Mary. May our journey continue beyond this pilgrimage, guided by the light of the Holy Spirit and protected under the mantle of Mary, our Mother. Amen.

Printed in Great Britain
by Amazon